THE NAKED CONSUMER TODAY

Jan Callebaut
Hendrik Hendrickx, Madeleine Janssens a.o.

The Naked Consumer Today
Or an overview of why consumers really buy things,
and what this means for marketing

Jan Callebaut
Hendrik Hendrickx, Madeleine Janssens a.o.
The Naked Consumer Today
Or an overview of why consumers really buy things,
and what this means for marketing
Antwerpen – Apeldoorn
Garant
2002

206 p. – 24 cm
D/2002/5779/115
ISBN 90-441-1358-5

Cover design: Walter Theunis
Cover illustration: Keppens Kreaties
Illustrations: Struyf & Partners
Editor: Susan Hrishenko

Garant Publishers
Somersstraat13-15, 2018 Antwerpen (Belgium)
Koninginnelaan 96, 7315 EB Apeldoorn (The Netherlands)
Coronet, 311 Bainbridge Street, Philadelphia PA 19147 (USA)
Central, 99 Wallis Road, London E9 5LN (England)

Contents

0. Introduction

Or an overview of why consumers really buy things, and what this means for marketing

Modern market research has made significant progress in pushing the envelope of analytical models of consumer behavior, but common and highly visible marketing failures indicate that something is missing in this approach. Long-term success in marketing requires an actionable understanding of consumer motivations. This Introduction details highlights of Censydiam's insights into these matters—ranging from the importance of the unconscious in consumer decision-making to the effective use of a universally applicable psychological model that can yield country-specific results.

• The case for motivational market research

Market research has a passionate love for analytics and quantification, especially in North America.

Since companies hire market research firms to make more money—generally by determining how much potential customers will buy if the company takes specific actions—this seems to be quite rational. Indeed, Censydiam believes that quantitative analysis is quite important, but it is often the wrong place to start with much market research when the goal is ongoing business success.

In the past few decades, market research has made impressive strides in creating advanced customer choice models based on a positivist view of human decision-making. Some of these models attempt to predict how much "utility" customers have for each element of a product. They also include ever more refined segmentation approaches that attempt to bridge the gap between describing customers in ways that make them easily targetable and describing *why* they engage in the buying behavior that they do. All of this work is very impressive in terms of analytical firepower.

Why, then, are there so many marketing failures? From the dawn of market research, why did the first car that was the product of extensive customer research—the Edsel—become a byword for failure? Why has New Coke become an abject lesson for misunderstanding what customers perceive in the products they buy? Why did Microsoft ever try to introduce *Microsoft Bob,* only to abandon him shortly thereafter? Why did one major beer brand in the United States come out with an advertisement whose subliminal message seemed to be "buy this beer or my dogs will kill you"? Why did an anti-speeding campaign in Belgium that used the time-honored approach of a sexy ad to gain attention result in more people actually speeding? Why did Apple Computer predicate a memorable ad campaign—a buff female athlete hurls a hammer at a large video monitor while an authoritarian figure pontificates in front of a crowd of suited figures—on anti-conformity when its (now failed) goal was to gain market share in big business? Not to mention all of the boring ads that compel no activity whatsoever, or the interesting ads that are memorable but generate limited buying activity. In general, why do most new products and line extensions fail?

As Disraeli said, "There are three types of lies. Lies, damnable lies, and statistics." We know that this is true. Just ask the apocryphal man who conducted market research on the milk market and determined that 50% of people like cold milk, while 50% like steamed milk, then decided to capture the market by promoting room temperature milk to everyone: the fallacy of the means. Analytics and precision are very important, but we must be quite certain that we are being precise about the correct issues.

In short, why are there so many marketing failures if market research is so compelling and insightful? Perhaps we are being very precise about the wrong questions.

• Don't mistake the trees for the forest

The answer is that there are all kinds of insight in the world. The first person who was able to determine that Alpha Centauri is exactly 4.3 light-years from the sun (Nicholas Louis de la Caille) was very insightful, but his insights rested upon the shoulders of the first person who looked up in the sky and said "You know, those are stars!"

More prosaically, consider results of a traditional market research study that revealed the average Dutch household does laundry seven times a week, while the average Belgian does wash four times a week. But what does this really tell us? Perhaps the Dutch are more fastidious, or have fewer clothes that need to be washed more often. Perhaps the Belgians have bigger washing machines, or water costs are higher so they wash more at one time. The facts themselves tell us almost nothing about how we should market such things as laundry detergent in these two countries.

Understanding the *what* in consumer purchase behavior—e.g. they will buy this many units of widgets at this price point—is very important. Price, however, is not a perfect indicator of value to a consumer. Air and water are extremely valuable, yet they are close to free in North America. It is possible to be grossly misled as to the intrinsic value consumers have for a product by how much they are actually paying, or willing to pay, for it at a specific point in time. *Understanding the* why, *however, is critical to repeatable marketing success.*

• Rational or rationalizing consumers?

Understanding *why,* however, is very challenging for the very Achilles'
heel that exists in most analytical approaches to market research—
customers are often more rationalizing than rational. That is why the
preponderance of consumers reading automotive ads have just bought
the car they are reading about. That is why people say they will behave
in one way, then behave in another. We know this: consumers are not
altogether rational in their reasons for buying products. Often they do
not fully understand the basis of their decisions themselves, so how can
they be expected to report them accurately to a market researcher?

This has been understood for some time, and has often been boiled
down to the idea that "sex sells." Well, sometimes it does, but using it
for all products in all circumstances is certainly a recipe for more
marketing failure.

In order to understand why people and companies buy things, it is often
necessary to delve into the realm of depth psychology—that form of
psychology that takes subconscious motivations seriously. (Yes, even
companies use some non-rational approaches to purchase decisions,
otherwise branding would not be so important in the corporate market.
Companies, after all, are made up of individuals.)

• A motivational market research parable

Consider our friend the Rhinoceros. By rights, he should be a happy
fellow. He is quite able to defend himself against the other animal
denizens. For humans, there are many tastier foods to eat than Rhino
meat.

And yet, our friend the Rhino has a serious problem. His horn is of avid
interest to many peoples in the world due to its special "properties."

Ask the average consumer about his or her interest in consuming what is
for all intents and purposes a powder composed of ground up dead
modified hair cells from a fairly unsanitary source, and the answer is
bound to be negative. Conduct a conjoint analysis on all of the
measurable physical attributes of this powder and you will have a very
precise measurement . . . of exactly the wrong question.

Instead, explore whether the average consumer would like to improve
his or her love life, and relate that human motivation to some *mystical*

aphrodisiac properties in a rhino's horn, and what you have is . . . a very panicked rhino. Does it matter that there is really no aphrodisiac in a rhino's horn? Unfortunately for the rhino, no. It only matters that there are enough interested buyers in the world to keep the rhino on the run.

Our friend the rhino is butting heads with the fact that consumer behavior is not truly rational. Consumer behavior is based on an attempt to satisfy deeply held needs. One of these needs is tied up in sexuality. There are several other primary needs as well. Adler tells us that these tend to be based on a combination of overcoming feelings of inferiority, and individual strategies to find satisfaction in life.

As consultants, we could advise Mr. Rhino in a host of marketing techniques to increase his "success." He could try to reposition his offering: "Touching live Rhino horns is so much more . . . stimulating." He could try to sell something else: *Viagra anyone*? He could remove his horn—*Ouch*! We suspect that he would not be all that interested in any of this, since our poor rhino does not want to be a product at all!

• The global consumer versus the rhino

From the marketers' perspective, one school of marketing would say that since everyone likes sex and many people relate a rhino's horn with improved sexual prowess, there should be a worldwide market for rhino horn if only the right global marketing efforts were brought to bear. In effect, this posits the "global consumer."

One could imagine ambitious American cattle farmers raising huge herds of rhinos. More efficient industrial animal farming techniques could be ramped up, while animal rights protesters stage sit-ins over the inhumane conditions to which all these penned rhinos are being subjected. Perhaps genetic engineering could develop larger, more robust rhino horns. Developing nations could turn to rhino farming to generate ready cash. Global advertising could extol the benefits of one rhino horn formulation and brand over another. The money would come rolling in.

But this is not to be. Everyone has an interest in sex, and yet only some very specific areas of the world seem to be interested in rhino horn. Most Westerners would be appalled at the idea of killing these creatures for such an end—especially since they do not believe that it will have the desired effect. Note that for some Eastern clientele, there is no need for scientific proof to underpin their belief in the efficacy of rhino horn. Indeed, in terms of their sexuality, who can say they are wrong? If they take rhino powder and their sexual experience improves, they would consider the product to be a good value.

Does this mean that there cannot be a uniform psychological model that motivational market researchers can use? Are Westerners uninterested in rhino horn because they are less interested in sex than some Easterners? Of course not!

The ancients, in the form of Plato, sought a uniformity in the "ideal" that was behind all of existence, and the commonality of the human

---

essence. Much of their quest for such things as justice was posited on how things ought to be. We moderns, however, have sought for the core of human motivations in psychoanalytical insight.

Human beings have fundamentally the same drives and motivations all over the world, but they are mediated and find expression through the prism of their geography and a host of other factors such as ethnicity and belief systems. In the East, many are interested in rhino powder. In the West, many would reach for Viagra. In the past, they might have reached for Spanish Fly.

This is what makes cross-cultural and multinational marketing so interesting and challenging. Even if a specific product can be marketed globally—and many are—the reasons that consumers would be interested in buying these product must be understood in terms of combining core human motivations and the context they live in.

• So what is a motivational market researcher to do?

The key to determining the correct questions to ask is psychodynamic market research. Its goal is to understand individuals within their specific "consumption environment," as opposed to just measuring consumption behavior.

Psychodynamic research does not initially provide numbers—but rather aims to provide a richer understanding of motivations and satisfaction strategies the consumer has in relation to specific products or brands.

This has the added benefit of laying the groundwork for superior analytical work at a later point.

This type of research can be conducted on a global basis because the fundamental basis of human nature really is the same around the world, even though specific cultural contexts may have a dramatic effect on buying behavior.

This all sounds very challenging. After all, individual psychoanalysis takes a very long time to show results, and market researchers have paying clients that demand fast, actionable results. Insight is required, but so are economies of scale in collecting these insights. It is not reasonable to have different researchers around the world using different psychological models to gather data concerning consumer motivations, then have them debate over the final meaning (as so often happens in academic circles).

The key is to have a compelling, uniform psychological model that can be deployed worldwide. This model should yield insight into common motivations among consumers as well as how these motivations are mediated in different cultures. The net result should be findings that enable a product announcement to factor in how things need to be positioned on a global basis for advertising and marketing, while taking into account regional differences. From New York to Ghana, from China to Australia, people have strikingly similar psychological needs. They are really part of the human condition. These needs, however, are mediated by their specific environment. Forget that, and invite marketing failure.

But how is such a model to be constructed?

• From Freud and Jung to Adler: why do consumers want to buy things?

Understanding the foundations of why consumers buy things can take us on a tour of the foundations of depth psychology.

It was Freud who brought to modernity the primary role of the unconscious in human motivations and actions. He also brought us a stark focus on Eros (e.g. sex) and Thanatos (e.g. the death instinct) as fundamental to understanding the role of the unconscious. From Freud, many marketers have latched onto the concept that "sex sells."

Jung departed from Freud in his focus on archetypes and the role of symbols in human consciousness and motivations. He also focused on the collective unconscious, wherein symbolic meaning could have a shared meaning across all human beings. From Jung, marketing has learned to look for universally understandable symbols that tap into the power of the collective unconscious.

Adler, with his focus on how people's motivations are grounded in different strategies for attempting to gain satisfaction in life—both individually and in the context of the social realm—yields the most actionable insights into human nature from a marketer's point of view.

• The power of motivational market research

Motivational market research is not an academic exercise, despite its academic underpinnings. As market researchers, we are interested in helping our clients be successful. By striving to fundamentally understand consumer motivations—instead of just measuring actual behavior or taking superficial answers to superficial questions at face value—we provide the ability for clients to create superior:

- Positioning, on a geographic and sub-segment basis
- Advertising
- Branding
- Product launches
- New product concepts
- Foundations for more traditional quantitative research

It is true that we live in a very quantitative age. Academics are more inclined to bemoan the lack of numerical literacy among our citizens than to advocate a better understanding of human nature. In terms of market research, this means that many studies leap to quantification too quickly.

People's motivations are not so easily put into an analytical black box. Quantification is ultimately necessary, but it is critical to understand the correct questions to ask before we attempt to become precise about consumers' buying dynamics.

This book attempts to lay a foundation for Censydiam's approach to Motivational Market Research with the following chapters:

1. *It all began in a zoo:* Censydiam thinks that marketing should not be reduced to simply marketing products. Marketing is about the strategy of facilitating desire. Marketing should not only speak to the desire for possessing utilitarian things such as fast-moving product and services, but also the desire of concepts and ideas. Marketing should help people reconcile themselves with their fellow men and with our world as such.

2. *The cornerstones:* The role of the unconscious is just as critical for consumers' buying decisions as it is for all other aspects of their lives. Our understanding of the key role of the unconscious has grown from Avicenna to Hegel to Freud. Most recently, Adler has laid out a compelling basis for understanding consumer psychology.

3. *A brief history of motivational market research:* Marketing's scientific roots descend from economics, but (as with economics) putting it on a positivist scientific footing may overstate the case. Effective marketing research attempts to ground its findings in

consumer psychology. This is the basis of *motivational market research.*

4. *The Censydiam model:* It is easy to observe and measure the overt rationales consumers use to justify purchases. As with an iceberg, however, the most powerful drivers of consumer satisfaction strategies lie beneath the surface. Censydiam's model yields a powerful tool to harness the insights of depth psychology for effective marketing.

5. *Conscious and unconscious:* The psychology of motives is critical to understanding consumer behavior. In a sense, this necessitates understanding the underpinnings of consumer imagination. The power of imagination consists not only of the power to make a representation based on a few impressions; it also consists of a world already constructed, based on the one that interprets these impressions. Marketing often communicates with symbols. A symbol can also call up reality. It does so, however, by means of a sometimes arbitrary code. How each consumer's imagination deals with these symbols is affected by his or her specific culture.

6. *The psychology of motives:* Product managers and marketers fail when they operate without a well-structured psychological understanding of consumer motivations. Every person has his or her own theory concerning why human beings think and act as they do. This theory is generally based on personal experience, but there is a global pattern of how consumers attempt to satisfy their needs. Effective marketers need to be aware of this pattern.

7. *Cross-culturally correct marketing:* Understanding human motivations is critical to success in marketing. The mechanisms of the human soul are universal, but because humans have different life stories, they also have different motivations. To discover motivations is the reason why we do motivational market research. Marketers have to understand motivations across cultures because they need to communicate with those motivations across different cultural contexts in order to be successful. There is no such thing as a homogenized, global consumer, despite the fact that psychological models can be universal.

8. *The Censydiam Illogic Algorithm:* Motivational market research is extremely challenging to conduct, but Censydiam's Illogic Algorithm is a unique tool that helps harness its complexity for our clients in a timely manner. The Censydiam Illogic Algorithm is a

computer program for interpretive analysis of consumer statements (gathered as text during interviews) and finding motivational clusters. It is based on our structural model of the underlying dimensions of consumer motivation.

9. *Future watch:* Professor Helmut Gaus has discovered long-term cyclical patterns of consumer "insecurity" that can be used to help forecast economic trends. His theory is rooted in the fact that a major part of our behavior is determined not by reason, but by subconscious processes. If we are forced to explain our behavior, we will hardly ever admit such a thing. Instead, we will try to find a rationalization. These unconscious processes, however, drive consumer behavior and can be used in aggregate to understand the antecedents of good and bad economic times.

10. *Four case studies:* Several case studies that illustrate the importance of the unconscious to consumer choice and hence motivational market research.

To the extent that consumption is fundamental to human society, why people buy what they buy is, in a sense, the fundamental question of modernity. It certainly gives significant insight into the human condition. Censydiam's approach gives our clients actionable insights that enable them to gain success in the marketplace.

Brad Bortner

1. It all began in a zoo

• (1): Marketing, a dirty word?

The title of our book reads: *The Naked Consumer Today.* You may be aware that there is another book with the title *The Naked Consumer,* and that is no coincidence. The latter book tells us about consumers who can no longer defend themselves—who stand "naked"—against marketing.

Indeed, in the eyes of many, marketing—and its direct product, advertising—is a dangerous, aggressive game; they say that it is a commercial war in which the innocent consumers are the victims.

One of their main objections is that marketing (and advertising) makes people buy things they do not want. It is, of course, the easiest objection one can make against marketing. Many people do buy things that, with hindsight, they did not want or—more correctly—things that did not make them happy.

What has happened then? There has been a communication breakdown between the marketing of that specific product and their expectations. It is as simple as that.

You the marketer and we the market researchers, are convinced of that, but how do we convince others? Unfortunately, it is not always as easy as it sounds to convince people—which is in fact one of the assignments of marketing.

A vicious circle? Misunderstandings all the way around?

Is marketing all about the relation between people and their commercial environment? No, it is much more than that. Marketing is a bridge between the consumer and the world around him—a world that is filled not only with commercial products, but also with ideas. In that sense, marketing has to play an ethical role in society. Ultimately, marketing should make people happy with better products, but also reconcile people with a better society in which they can feel happy.

We will come back to that later, but let us first reconstruct a conversation that may sound familiar to you, as a marketer.

• (2): A little bit immoral?

"Oh, so you're into market research. You scrutinize what happens in the marketplace—what people buy."

"Why yes, but we do a little more than that. We try to find out, for instance, *why* people buy specific things," I said.

"Does anyone really want to know why? Isn't it enough to know that they *are* buying those things? Won't that make the manufacturer happy? Do they really need market researchers to know that?"

"Some manufacturers happen to want to know *why* consumers buy their products, too."

"You're telling me that they don't know why people buy their stuff? That's ridiculous! People don't buy a TV set just to listen to the radio!"

"Well, people who want to listen to musical programs will want to buy a stereo TV set. Still, TV manufacturers already know that, too. *We* tell them what things people expect from their TV sets. We tell them *which* people buy a TVset to listen to music, and *which* ones buy TVs to watch shows, or soaps, or news, and *why* they do so. And also whether it could be of interest to manufacture TV sets to . . . just listen to."

"Next you'll tell the TV stations what they should broadcast too!"

"If they ask us, we sure will. That is, we will tell the broadcasters what people expect from a TV station, which is an entirely different thing. We will help broadcasters give the public what they are looking for."

"Looking? Or listening? Are you speaking literally or figuratively now?"

"Figuratively, of course. Whether they will literally look will depend upon the programs. We can do many things, but we don't make TV programs—yet."

"Are you actually trying to make more people watch TV or make better TV programs?"

"If TV offers better programs, programs people will want to see, then more people will watch TV. And more people will feel content with the shows. We do not want more viewers; we want more contented viewers."

"Oh, come on, lay off! You just want to sell more, the lot of you. You want people to buy things they don't need. Isn't that just a little bit immoral?"

• (3): Do we live on bread alone?

"Do you think we only buy things we need? You just rang me up on your latest mobile phone. Couldn't you have called me from a pay phone?" I asked.

"Pay phones should exist; they are a social necessity for people who don't have a cell phone. I happen to have one. My cell phone is my freedom. Don't tell me that you tricked me into buying it with your marketing sweet-talk."

"Aren't you contradicting yourself now? You just said that we marketing people are responsible for people buying things they don't need. What is it that people really need?"

"Bread. And water."

"All right, bread and water. Let us . . ."

"As a matter of fact, the thing about bread comes from the prayer: *Give us this day our daily bread*."

"You see? That is a good example of marketing before the term existed. Today, you'll see some bakeries with *Our Daily Bread* painted on their windows. But let's go back to water. Why do you think people buy more water these days?"

"Do they? You mean bottled water. Not just ordinary water. Because... bottled water has something extra."

"So people are not content with water alone, without any extras?"

"Extras? Most of those bottles contain spring water, and since most people do not have a spring in their backyard . . ."

"You don't say! Could it be that mineral water in a bottle is the same water from a spring that, as it happens, does not gurgle up in your backyard? Let's talk about bread then. Aside from the fact that our prayers ask for daily bread, people eat less and less ordinary bread. People breakfast on croissants and cereals now. This daily bread of yours seems not to satisfy them completely. People want more, and they want something different."

"Then you should do something to change that immediately!"

"Why, if people don't want just ordinary bread anymore?"

"People should want it, they must want it! Bread is good for your health, bread is the symbol of life, bread is . . ."

"Okay. We will put you on bread and water for a week, along with your cell phone. Just give me a ring on the eighth day and tell me if water and bread is life itself. You can also call me from a pay phone, if it suits you better."

• (4): A strategy of desire

A tongue-in-cheek defense of marketing? The way we at Censydiam see it, we have nothing to defend. Marketing is not the source of all evil in the world; marketing is the source of interactive coexistence.

It is impossible to imagine life today without marketing. However, we think that marketing should not be reduced to marketing products. Marketing should create new forms of relationships.

Marketing is a strategy of desire. Marketing should create the desire of possessing utilitarian things such as fast-moving products and services, but should also create the desire of concepts and ideas. Marketing should create people's desire to reconcile themselves with their fellow men and with our world as such.

Marketing should be the strategy of desire that takes the place of ideologies and ideological systems, which can, as we have recently seen, become the real threat to harmonious relationships in our world. Then, and only then, is marketing ethically sound and justified.

Why should governments and administrations not use marketing to convince—no, to explain how they see the welfare of our society? Why should they thus not create the desire of living one's life in such a society?

When Censydiam was established, this was our motive, our motivation. Starting from psychology and sociology, we saw not only products and commerce, we saw the whole man (the "naked" man) and all his desires, and not only his immediate needs or wishes. We wanted to fulfill more than that. We looked at man not only from outside in, but also from inside out.

Did it all begin in a zoo? Oh, yes. Our first assignment as the *founding fathers* of what was to become a multinational corporation was the local zoo of Antwerp. We did not think of selling more tickets or subscriptions in the first place. We looked at the zoo as a human experience and not—as had been the case until then—as an educational institution. We "marketed" the zoo as a human experience people would want, would "desire" to visit, not to see the animals and make the zoo richer but to enrich themselves. It worked. The Antwerp Zoo is still in full swing, thank you very much.

Jan Callebaut and Hendrik Hendrickx

2. The cornerstones

Or how psychoanalysis taught us to go deeper
than the surface of consumerism

The role of the unconscious is just as critical for consumers' buying
decisions as it is for all other aspects of their lives. Our understanding of
the key role of the unconscious has grown from Avicenna to Hegel to
Freud. Most recently, Adler has laid out a compelling basis for
understanding consumer psychology.

• Avicenna (1): The real "inventor" of the subconscious

Sigmund Freud was not the first to discover the structure of the conscious and the unconscious mind; before Freud, Hegel gave the unconscious an important role in his philosophy. The real discovery, however, dates back to the early Middle Ages when the Arabic scholar Avicenna first mentioned the subconscious in his Canon of Medicine.

No, it was not at Berggasse 19 in Vienna that the subconscious was "invented." It was not Dr. Sigmund Freud who first mentioned the existence of an unconscious part of the mind. Before Freud, Hegel gave the unconscious an important role in his philosophy. The unconscious, the stuff that philosophy is made of—is it all in the mind? What does the unconscious, or subconscious, actually do? Does it play a role in our lives or is it just sitting there, mysteriously hidden?

Dr. Freud discovered—or rather rediscovered, as we shall see—that the unconscious could influence behavior and bodily functions. But everything needed to be figured out. How was the unconscious structured? What were its dynamics? Freud gave us the answers. The physician became the psychoanalyst.

Yet it was not the Viennese doctor, but another physician who first described what we call the structure of the conscious and the unconscious mind. It was Abu 'Ali al-Husain ibn Sina, known in the West as Avicenna. The year? Around 1000 AD.

Avicenna's life reads like a story from the *Tales of the Thousand and One Nights*. He was born in Bukhara—now in Uzbekistan—in 980 AD. He received his first education from his father, an Isma'ili, a member of an Islamic religious and political movement that drew its philosophy from the Greek Neoplatonists. We will have to remember that. It is important for understanding Avicenna's later views.

Avicenna was a precocious child with an exceptional memory. He had memorized the Koran and much of the Arabic poetry of his times by theage of ten. Thereafter, he studied logic and philosophy under teachers whom he soon outgrew, and medicine.

After a period of wandering, he became court physician at Hamadan. There he enjoyed the favor of the ruler, prince Shams ad-Dalah, who twice appointed him vizier.

This was the period when he began compiling his two most famous works, *The Book of Healing* and *The Canon of Medicine*.

• Avicenna (2): Soul-in-body or the "global man"

Avicenna introduced the philosophy of Aristotle and Plotinus into Arab culture. According to Plotinus, the wisdom in the universe—the first emanation of the One, or God—illuminates the world throughout all stages of its hierarchy. In Man, there is the conscious activity of a "higher soul" and less conscious feelings of the "lower soul," the first hint at the subconscious level of the soul.

We must not imagine Avicenna as a scholarly recluse, sitting at his desk in his study.

Occupied during the day with his duties at court as both physician and administrator, Avicenna spent almost every night with his students, composing his works and discussing philosophical and scientific issues with them.

They combined these sessions with musical performances and gaiety that lasted late into the night.

It was through Avicenna that the Greek philosophy of Aristotle became an integral part of Arabic culture. Avicenna made Aristotle's philosophy the foundation of his personal, original system. He also found inspiration in a group of Plotinian texts that had passed into Arabic under the title of *Theology of Aristotle.*

Why not just use Aristotle directly? Well, Plotinus was a Rationalist. He paid respect to *nous,* or wisdom. However, in Plotinus' view, that is the wisdom in the universe and the first emanation of the One, which is supreme. This was an idea that particularly pleased the Muslim world. The One, of course, could be identified with Allah.

According to Plotinus, this wisdom illuminates the world throughout all stages of its hierarchy: the One, the wisdom, the soul, the soul-in-body, and matter. Man, who is soul-in-body, can strive by rational means to understand what is above him. He may grasp the rationality of the world.

Plotinus held that conscious activity (cognition) by a "higher soul" depended on data from the senses. On the other hand, physical sensations, passions, and feelings were seen as passive states of the "lower soul." Here we have a first hint at the subconscious level of the soul.

Let us go back now to Avicenna and see how he described man as soul-in-body, how he described "global man."

• Avicenna (3): Body and soul are a whole

In Avicenna's work, body and soul form a complete whole—one single being. The soul refers to the corporeal soul, i.e. the power that originates understanding. It is a natural faculty that arises from a higher order than the animal faculty. Anger, fear, and similar emotions are passions from the same faculty, the "apprehensive faculty."

We can classify the views on how we gain knowledge of the world under three headings.

The first—the *Platonic* view—regards the human being as "soul within the body," while admitting "soul" to be indefinable and beyond the power of location.

The second—the *scientific* or rationalistic and modern view—takes the physical body as the fundamental, seeing in it the outcome of known or at least knowable forces. The facts of anatomy, physiology, etc., convey their own inevitable conclusions. This view, of course, is the most appealing. One feels one can grasp some tangible knowledge.

There is, however, a third view—the so-called *scholastic* view we inherited from Saint Thomas and his followers. It says: "It is not my soul that thinks, or my body that eats, but 'I' that do both." In other words, again: *The body and "soul" form a complete whole—one "single being."*

It is this view that Avicenna inaugurated, long before the Thomists, in his *Canon of Medicine*. It is the view that makes the ancient work fall in line with the most "modern."

When the ancients use the word "soul," Avicenna writes, they refer to the earthly or corporeal soul, the source of all those faculties upon which the movements and various bodily operations depend. It is the power that originates understanding and voluntary movement. It is a natural faculty that arises from a higher order than the animal faculty in medicine.

Anger, fear, and similar emotions are passions of the same faculty, and admittedly arise from the senses, the judgment, i.e. the apprehensive faculty. The seat of this faculty, says Avicenna, is the mid-portion of the brain. It combines or separates, as the mind selects, those particular perceptions that are stored in the imagination and are founded on common sense.

This faculty belongs partly to the intellectual imagination and partly to the rational (or ratiocinative) faculty, the understanding.

• Avicenna (4): The sense of what makes for well-being

In animals, the "apprehensive faculty" is called instinct. On many occasions, Man uses it exactly as does an irrational animal. Avicenna situates it partly in the higher and in the lower soul, exactly as Jung will situate the "instinct" between the conscious and unconscious level of the soul. Avicenna prefigured the role of willpower, too, and thus hinted at Adler's "willing being."

This faculty—Avicenna calls it the "Apprehensive Faculty"—is the instrument of the power called *instinct* in animals. By it, for instance, an animal knows that a wolf is an enemy. Such a decision is not formed by the reasoning powers. Friendship and enmity are not perceived by the senses and they are not perceived by reason either.

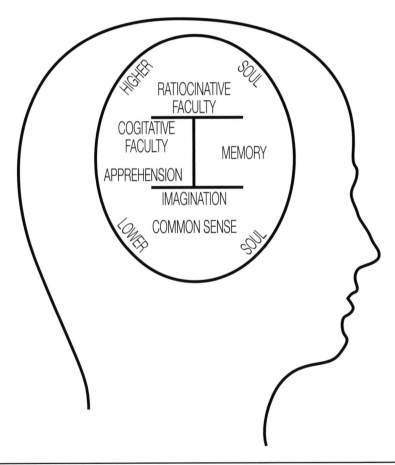

Man employs the same "apprehensive faculty" on very many occasions exactly as does an irrational animal.

Clearly, Avicenna's "apprehensive faculty" covers both "lower soul" or lower reason and "higher soul" or reason as ordinarily understood. The former is also called instinct. Ten centuries later, Carl Gustav Jung will situate the "instinct" between the conscious and the unconscious level of the soul.

The fact that feelings, imagination, and thoughts influence character is of the greatest importance, but by using the willpower to control them all, one becomes also master of one's life and "fate." This is what makes for the sense of well-being in the individual, says Avicenna.

The attitude of our mind can be overruled by the will. Do we perceive here the prototype of Alfred Adler's "willing being?"

Avicenna has thus not only prefigured Freud's theories about the different levels of the soul, but also Jung's instincts and Adler's fundamental role of the will.

• Freud (1): The Movie

Sigmund Freud, the father of psychoanalysis, who did not "invent" the subconscious but invented the word for it, has always been and still is a larger-than-life figure, the stuff that dreams are made of. And indeed, Freud first used dreams to explore the unconscious.

Though he hinted at the existence of a subconscious part of the mind, Avicenna never invented the word "unconscious."

Theologians—Christian as well as Islamic—find it difficult to accept the concept of the subconscious mind. It would imply that Man has no free will. Philosophers also find it difficult: it lowers Man to the rank of an animal, an animal with instinct instead of logical reasoning. Medicine—until Freud's times—rejected the idea.

With the nonprofessional, however, the subconscious has always enjoyed certain popularity. It was the stuff that dreams were made of. And indeed, Freud wrote a fat book on the interpretation of dreams. It had nothing in common with popular dream reading but it became Freud's most popular work.

Doubtless this popularity was the main reason why John Huston wanted to make a movie about Sigmund Freud. Huston himself did not believe in the subconscious; he believed in the spectacle of hypnosis. He was an outstanding parlor hypnotist, which comes in very handy for a moviemaker, who has to hypnotize the masses.

It was Sartre, of all people, whom Huston asked to write the script. At that time, the pope of existentialism enjoyed popularity almost equal to that of the pope of psychoanalysis. He also did not believe in the unconscious. Sartre believed the subconscious stood in the way of personal freedom.

Collaboration between Sartre and Huston did not run very smoothly to say the least. Sartre's script would have resulted in a movie lasting no less than . . . seven hours. Huston wanted to reduce it to Hollywood proportions. Huston—who pretended not to have an unconscious of his own, but at the same time told Sartre his most obviously Oedipal dreams—wanted to drown Sartre in a torrent of words as if winning an argument against Sartre was more important than making a movie about Freud. The only thing he forgot was that Sartre did not understand a word of what he said. Sartre did not speak English.

• Freud (2): Conscious and unconscious,
   the properties of the contents of the mind

According to Freud, the mind is composed of three parts: the Id, the Ego, and the Superego. The Id, the Ego, and the Superego function in different levels of consciousness. The interaction among the three functions represents a constant movement of items from one level to another.

Eventually, Huston did make his movie, *Freud* (1962), but we can hardly recommend the movie as an introduction to Freud's scientific methods. Unfortunately, Sartre's original script was never published.

There are many excellent books on Freud. You can find everything you want to know about Freud in Ernest Jones' *Sigmund Freud, Life and Work*, and in the more recent and ultimate two-volume history of psychoanalysis, Elisabeth Roudinesco's *Histoire de la psychanalyse*, which is also available in English.

Let us confine ourselves to some basic elements that are minimal for a better understanding of the methods we use.

According to Freud, the human mind is composed of three parts: the Id, the Ego, and the Superego.

So Freud did not divide the human mind into the conscious and the unconscious? Not exactly, no. The mental processes can proceed along three—not two—levels of consciousness: the conscious level, ruled by the Ego; the preconscious; and the unconscious. However, the conscious, the preconscious, and the unconscious are not designated as parts of the structure of the human mind as such, but only as properties of conceptions or of contents of the mind.

The Id, the Ego, and the Superego function in different levels of consciousness. Indeed, Freud's theory of the mind hinges upon the ability of impulses or memories to "float" from one level to another.

The interaction among the three functions of the mind represents a constant movement of items from one level to another. It also means that the motivational forces can "float" from the unconscious to the conscious. And we will show you how we deal with those different levels in our research.

But first let us get acquainted with the Id, the Ego, and the Superego...

• Freud (3): The Id, the source of immediate urges and needs

For the baby, the womb has been the perfect supermarket. In this ideal supermarket, all the demands of its Id—its wishes, urges and needs—have been satisfied immediately. As a baby in the womb, we are in a state of total satisfaction. When we come into the world, it is a different question: we must develop our own ways of coping with it.

We have our lives lived—being driven—by unknown, uncontrolled forces, says Freud. These forces reside in what Freud has called the Id. In psychoanalytic theory, the Id is one of the three basic elements of personality, the others being the Ego and the Superego.

The Id is ruled by the *pleasure principle*. We can say that the Id is obeying the mute but mighty Thanatos, which wants to quiet the interfering Eros at the signals of the pleasure principle.

The Id can be equated with the unconscious itself, although it is the most accessible part of the personality. In addition to the different drives, the Id also encloses repressed mental content.

The Id consists of drives and impulses that can be satisfied, such as hunger, thirst, security, and so on. The Id also contains the whole range of aggressive instincts and urges. Moral and ethical values are alien to the Id.

The Id ignores reality and time. It ignores realistic obstacles just like a child in a crowded elevator impulsively wants to go to the lavatory. Indeed, the Id will not stand for a delay in gratification.

The Id is always active and searches for satisfaction. If satisfaction is not immediately obtained, it endangers the balance of the Ego, as the Ego has to reconcile the urges of the Id and adapt it to the outer world

How that will be done is one of the most important questions in motivational marketing research.

• Freud (4): The Ego, the pragmatic satisfaction of needs

The eventual understanding that immediate gratification is usually impossible comes with the formation of the Ego, which is ruled by the reality principle. Whereas the Id may have an urge and form a picture that satisfies this urge, the Ego engages in a strategy to actually fulfill the urge and eventually builds a great number of skills and memories to help us repeat these strategies.

We are born into a divided world—a world in which the source of our needs has been separated from the source of satisfaction—and, growing up, we must develop ways of coping with this dilemma.

How do we do this? What part of our personality is responsible for it?

The Ego is the seat of the *reality principle*. The Ego functions intelligently and supports the Id. For example, the Ego knows that a can contains food. It knows how to open the can and eat the food, whereas the Id only knows hunger that has to be satisfied.

The Ego tries to use the outside world to satisfy the Id. It is, in fact, under the influence of the outside world that the Id has been modeled: the Ego is the control mechanism of the conscious. The Ego represents reason and common sense, which will assert the rights of the reality principle over the Id's pursuit of pleasure.

Part of the Ego is unconscious. We are not always aware of the control the Ego exerts on the Id. Freud compared the Ego with a person on horseback who leads the animal—the Id.
In fact, the Ego is part of the Id that developed and acquired reason and intelligence, and rules the Id with its control function, but must also preserve it from the outside world.

With the formation of the Ego, the individual becomes a self, instead of an amalgamation of urges and needs.

Becoming a self means that we will all have different solutions, different ways of coping with dilemmas. Translated into marketing terms, it means that we will not only have different buying behaviors, but different motivations steering that behavior. Finding out the how and why will be our main task.

• Freud (5): The Superego, the rulebook

The Superego is the person's "good conscience"; the word itself tells us that all this takes place in consciousness. And what is the unconscious then? The unconscious holds all that is repressed and also remainders of older stages of development.

The Ego is governed not only by drives and practical necessities, but also by the question of whether behaviors are allowed according to inner standards. This self-considering attitude or inner conscience is called the Superego. It contains the rules and precepts of parents and other authorities as well as the Ego ideal the individual himself developed, i.e. the sort of person he or she would like to be.

However, if a person does something that is acceptable to the Superego, he experiences pride and self-satisfaction. This is the Ego ideal. The Ego ideal aims the individual's path of life toward the ideal, perfect goals instilled by society. We will have to remember that when we discuss Alfred Adler.

And the unconscious in all that? Consciousness is not the essence of the mental: it is the quality of it. It is situated on the border between the inner man and the outside world.

The unconscious mental content is that which is prevented from being lifted into consciousness, particularly the repressed content: what is repressed is unconscious.

The unconscious, however, also holds material other than that which is repressed. There we also find older remainders of an earlier stage of development of evolving living creatures, in which the unconscious was the only level on which mental phenomena occurred: the beast in Man. The unconscious contains mental material that we know directly through its effects. The unconscious primarily contains the greater part of the Id and the deepest strata of the Superego.

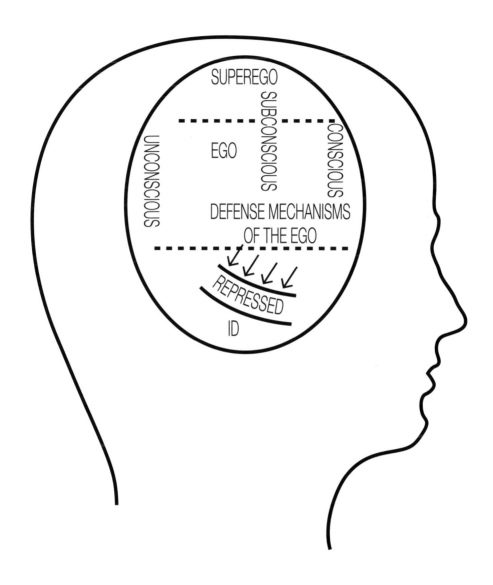

• Freud (6): Defense mechanisms and buying behavior

Suppression is pushing unacceptable impulses into the unconscious. The suppressed facts express themselves in a disguised form: the representations and feelings embodied by the drives. Sublimation directs unacceptable impulses into acceptable social forms. These defense mechanisms play an important role in a commercial environment.

The two main defense mechanisms of the Ego are suppression and sublimation.

Suppression is pushing unwanted impulses (and later, unwanted ideas and thoughts, too) into the unconscious.

The suppressed facts do not remain imperceptible, but express themselves in a disguised form. The drives themselves have not been suppressed, only the representations and the feelings embodied by the drives.

Any form of behavior, such as buying behavior, can express these drives. Insight into the stereotypical suppressed content will give the market researcher the chance to play along with it harmoniously as the suppressed needs ask for expression.

Sublimation is directing unacceptable impulses into acceptable and perfected social forms. Drives as they are, they blindly pursue objects from which they can expect normal satisfaction. To sublimate these drives, they have to be suppressed by the Ego, which builds defense mechanisms against them.

One does not need unbridled imagination to recognize particular buying behavior as aggression against parents, proceeding from a submissive childhood situation, in a sublimated form.

Young people, for example, wanting modern design in contrast with their parents' classical furniture. Or young girls rebelling against their mothers' weight control—expressed by a predilection for so-called light products—falling back on the richness of butter. As we will see later, these rather simplistic examples are obviously more subtly present in a commercial environment.

• Jung (1): The structure of the personality

Jung's understanding of the unconscious was subtler than Freud's: there was a personal unconscious—a whole of forgotten and suppressed matter, some we can easily recall to consciousness—and a collective unconscious, containing matter acquired by humanity's ancestry—a core that cannot be made conscious. Jung's unconscious is anything but the dark chaos Freud has described.

Following Freud, Jung pictured conscious and unconscious levels and a mental energy source called libido. Like Freud, he wanted to make the unconscious accessible. Apart from that, they differed radically.

Jung tried to be more comprehensive and more purposeful. Unlike most of his colleagues, Jung never believed that science and religion were incompatible.

The unconscious. Jung's understanding of the subconscious was much subtler than Freud's. There was a personal subconscious of vague memories and suppressed knowledge, and a collective unconscious on a lower level, which resulted from uncontrolled emotions and visions. The unconscious makes it possible for the conscious to function better: the individual draws inspiration from it to compensate and restore the mental balance. To Jung, the unconscious is not exclusively pathogenic.

The personal unconscious. The personal unconscious is a whole of forgotten and suppressed material accumulated during a lifetime. It consists of the preconscious and of the unconscious. The preconscious contains impressions of memories and associations that we can easily recall; the unconscious contains all sorts of forgotten material that we can recall to consciousness.

As for content, the personal unconscious holds but a small part of the driving force of human personality. It is situated in the collective unconscious.

The collective unconscious. Jung refers to it as the inherited possibility to function mentally. It contains material that has been acquired by humanity's ancestry: instincts that are common to the whole species, the archetypes, and finally the deepest and unreachable level. A core that cannot be made conscious: the sediment of our forebears' experiences.

This human heritage has nothing in common with the dark chaos of impulses as Freud sees them. Jung's unconscious has a primeval structure and a primeval organization, like a burial chamber filled with priceless treasures that begin to glow in the light of the consciousness exploring the darkness of the tomb.

• Jung (2): The archetypes and symbolism, or Jung vs. Freud

Archetypes are the self-portraits of the instincts. They are the lighting systems of our thoughts, feelings, representations, and knowledge. Proof of their existence lies in the fact that pathological motives and dream symbols are comparable all over the world. It would be wonderful for marketers if they could connect their commercial messages with these universal signs and symbols.

The term *archetypes* was first used by Saint Augustine, referring to the fundamental principles of human nature.

According to Jung, they are primitive mental processes that are converted into images that consciousness can understand, even if only by way of symbols and metaphors. Archetypes are the self-portraits of the instincts. They are the lighting systems of our thoughts, feelings, representations, and knowledge.

Jung sees *proof of the existence of archetypes* in the fact that various pathological motives and dream symbols are comparable all over the world. This applies also for many forms of religious expression. Examples are: water, fire, the hero, the witch, the father, the mother, the slain and resurrected god, et cetera. An immense treasure of elements which again and again allow the mind to make new discoveries.

The *functional significance of symbols* has been clearly demonstrated throughout history. Religious symbols, for example, thus appear to be efficient guides to moral conduct.

Freud interprets the symbols in a semiotic manner, i.e. as a sign or expression of psychosexual processes. Jung, for whom Freud's sexual theory was an unproven hypothesis, attributes a historical value to these symbolic manifestations. Their meaning is to be found in their significance for the actual and future experiences of the psyche.

From a communicative point of view, it would be wonderful for marketers if they could connect their commercial messages with this collection of signs and symbols found in the collective unconscious, which, consequently, will be interpreted in the same way by vast groups of consumers in various cultures. Cross-cultural marketing is one of the challenges of today's multinational companies, which sell their goods all over the world.

- Jung (3): The conscious and the unconscious Ego, or alter ego, and the Self

The real center of the personality is the Self, situated in the center of the field of the unconscious. Man must undergo a process of individuation, a mental maturing process of the Self. Only then can the Self come into being, only then can we really relate with others.

According to Jung, the personality consists of two parts: the conscious and the unconscious parts. The center of consciousness is the Ego. The center of the unconscious is the shadow of the Ego: the alter ego, the unconscious Ego. This is the unconscious counterpart of the Ego, which can to some extent give an unconscious compensation for immoral forms of satisfaction of the Ego.

The Ego is situated in the center of the field of the unconscious. Therefore, the real center of the personality is indeed the Self. Consciousness cannot directly understand the Self, but only express it by symbols that sum up the whole of the conscious and the unconscious.

Jung says that man must undergo a process of individuation, a mental maturing process of the Self. Jung applies this individuation to the psyche as well as to human relations. Only the individuated persona can really relate with others.

When the psyche reaches full maturity, the Self can come into being. It is the realization of the Self that leads man to the development of the individual psyche as a being that can be distinguished from the collective psyche.

Individuation is achieved in two stages. The Ego must identify with the Self, and the Self, although part of the deepest coexistence, must reach its own highest possible and separate development.

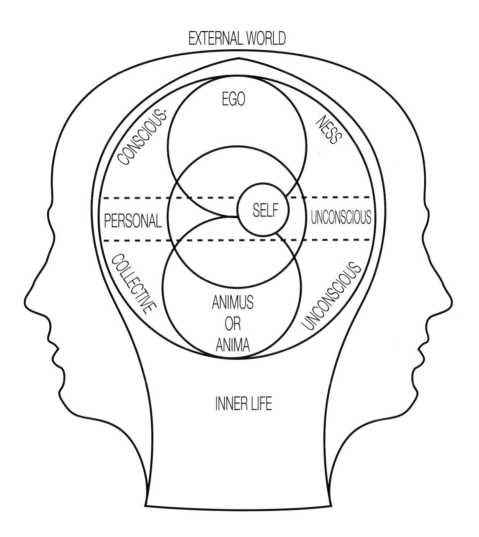

EXTERNAL WORLD

EGO

CONSCIOUS-

NESS

SELF

PERSONAL

UNCONSCIOUS

COLLECTIVE

ANIMUS
OR
ANIMA

UNCONSCIOUS

INNER LIFE

• Jung (4): The functions of the psyche

The psyche has four functions: thinking and feeling, sensation and intuition. Most people have a preferred function, with at least one accessory function. The conscious and unconscious parts of the psyche are divided not only between these four functions: they are also polarized between two attitudes, extroversion and introversion.

To Jung, the psyche has four further functions: *thinking and feeling, sensation and intuition.* These are forms of mental activities that are disconnected from the content. The axis thinking/feeling requires insight. The axis sensation/intuition requires perception. The poles are opposed insofar as one pole forever cancels the other out for a while, though both can in turn be used as alternatives.

Most people have a preferred function, with at least one accessory function. That is why the empiricist will focus on *thinking*, the theorist on *intuition*, the aesthete on *feelings*, and the sensualist on *sensations*. The conscious and unconscious parts of the psyche are divided not only between those four functions, they are also polarized between two attitudes: extroversion and introversion.

Extroversion is characterized by a more positive relation with the outside world (extroverts are talkative and sociable); introverts have a more positive relation with their inner life (pensive and reclusive). The functions of thinking and feeling, of sensation and intuition can thus be directed inwards or outwards.

In general, the unconscious completes the consciousness: a quiet and intuitive introvert often hides a noisy, sensual extrovert who may break loose in strenuous circumstances.

Incidentally, this is what happened to Jung himself when he embarked upon a psychic self-exploration that some considered a breakdown and that Jung himself called a "confrontation with the unconscious."

However, Jung emerged from the ordeal with renewed conviction of his theory on archetypes, the collective unconscious, and the process of individuation. Jung had found out at the cost of slipping down into psychosis.

- Jung (5): The Persona, or Self-image, and its antipode, the animus or anima

Although Jung's description of the mechanisms of the psyche is much richer than Freud's, it does not help us marketers much to understand the motivations that govern needs and desires as to the consumers' decision-making processes and buying behavior. For this, Adler is important.

When the Ego uses a dominant function in its contacts with the outside world, it will develop a *persona* as a marginal characteristic. The persona is a self-image the individual presents to the outside world as a reality. This facade is a compromise among the Ego as it would like to be, the social functions it must perform, and the limitations intrinsic to the situation in life. The ideal case is the persona as a resilient, protective coating, smoothing over the daily confrontations. If the elements with which the persona is formed are not balanced, the persona grows into a stereotyped mask.

The *anima* is the remnant of feminine nature in the unconscious of the male (feminine affects). The animus is the masculine element that is unconsciously present in feminine nature (the need to act, masculine ways of reacting).

According to Jung, the male is primarily characterized by thinking and observing, and women by feeling and intuition. The male suppresses the woman within himself and the woman suppresses the man within herself. The subconscious in men as well as in women finds a compensatory factor in these respective feminine and masculine elements.

Although Jung's description of the mechanisms of the psyche is much richer than Freud's, it does not help us marketers much to understand the lines of force, the motivations that govern needs and desires in the matter of the consumers' decision-making processes and buying behavior.

Adler's *Individualpsychologie* is somewhat simpler than Freud's and Jung's theories as it introduces fewer, but otherwise truly important, concepts and principles. Concepts and principles that are important to us for building a frame of reference we can rely on in our motivational market research.

• Adler (1): Individual Psychology and its social perspective

The individual is not internally divided, nor is he the battleground of conflicting forces. There is a future-oriented striving toward a goal of significance, superiority, or success, called the striving for superiority. Moreover, the theory of Adler mentions the existence of a community spirit. We will call it "belonging."

Alfred Adler's *Individualpsychologie* is a view of the relation of man's individual Ego with his own corporeality, with the entire psyche of the individual and with the community of the others.

This holistic view makes it especially interesting to use as a starting point for developing a frame of reference for consumer behavior. This is what Censydiam did and we will explain it later. But let us first explain what Adler's *Individualpsychologie* is all about.

According to Adler, the individual is neither internally divided, nor is he the battleground of conflicting forces. There is a consistent pattern of dealing with life. There is one central personality dynamic derived from the growth and forward movement of life itself. It is a future-oriented striving toward a goal of significance, superiority, or success.

Adler recognizes a *striving for superiority* in which the affirmation of others and the power struggle against others are manifest. He also mentions the existence of a community spirit and an effective social interest that we will call *belonging*.

The basis of Adler's theory is *Organ Inferiority*. As a child, even a healthy person is strongly influenced by his bodily inferiority as opposed to adults. In comparison with adults, the child is inevitably weaker. This means that for the rest of one's life, one will seek to overcome the feelings of inferiority brought on by these earliest experiences.

Through compensation of earlier feelings of inferiority, every human being develops a craving for power. Ultimately, every individual develops his own lifestyle to handle problems that arise from interaction with others. According to Adler, an ideal lifestyle leads to a creative and positive approach that allows the individual to direct his capacities toward constructive goals.

• Adler (2): Dealing with Organ Inferiority

The experience of Organ Inferiority causes unpleasant feelings the individual can react to in two ways. The (stereotype) masculine way of reacting is by compensating. The (stereotype) feminine way of reacting is characterized by passiveness and defeatism, or reconciling oneself with one's inferiority. Adler coined the expression "inferiority complex."

The experience of Organ Inferiority is the central and decisive point in man's life. By Organ Inferiority, Adler meant the objectively or subjectively less or not functioning of a particular organ or part of the body. Objectively: stuttering, a cleft palate, bad sight or hearing, a malformed face or part of the body. Subjectively: organs or parts of the body that function normally but are experienced by the individual as inferior to those of older or stronger people. It is important to point out that an inferior organ or part of the body—which are in fact only partial defects—exert their influence on the individual's entire psyche.

The experience of Organ Inferiority causes unpleasant feelings for which a solution must be found. The individual can react in two ways.

The (stereotypical) masculine reaction is to compensate. This means not reconciling oneself with the real or imaginary malfunctioning of the organ or part of the body, but trying to reach a normal or higher functional level.

The (stereotypical) feminine reaction is characterized by passiveness and defeatism. Reconciling oneself with one's inferiority. When this feeling deeply affects the psyche, Adler speaks of an inferiority complex or insecurity and inferiority which spans several areas of life and distorts behavior and reactions. As for consumer behavior, this can lead to the rejection of particular brands as *too good for me, beyond my means,* or also as *too masculine.* Conversely, the masculine way of reacting leads to buying a particular product or brand that is compensatory for the inferiority one feels, e.g. women who choose to smoke cigars.

Adler makes a further distinction between real and unreal compensation. Compensation is real when the goals are realistic and socially valuable. Unreal compensation is socially negative compensation, such as a husband who cowers before his wife at home, but compensates for his domestic inferiority by browbeating his colleagues at work.

- Adler (3): Coping with inferiority feelings:
  masculine protest or resignation

Masculine protest and resignation—in men as well as women—can reflect in buying behavior. Let us not forget that in this context, "masculine" and "feminine" ways of reacting are not gender-linked; the psyche is neutral.

This striving for superiority, proceeding from the experience of inferiority, is instilled during childhood. The young child thinks highly of physical strength and control, especially the child who is hampered by constitutional inferiority or who grows up in difficult circumstances—because external or internal inhibitions prevent satisfaction of the needs. The child forms an image of the world founded on threats and hostility, and will develop a high degree of aggressiveness or assertiveness.

Adler sees human relations chiefly from the perspective of a struggle. In our Western world, the male is endowed with the symbolism of power and active dominance. Here again, in parallel with Organ Inferiority, two attitudes regarding life are possible: masculine protest or resignation.

In Adler's *Individualpsychologie*, masculine protest means the tendency—in men as well as women—to cope with feelings of inferiority in an active way and thereby suppress feminine or feminine-like tendencies. Stubbornness, dominance, ambition, and aggressiveness are examples of masculine protest. In daily life, it can hide behind attitudes such as swearing, exaggeratedly clearing one's throat, or, as far as women are concerned, riding a motorcycle, heavy smoking, driving a car in a masculine way, and so on.

The opposite, of course, is resignation. Obedient resignation and submission are further characterized by constantly expressing a need for appreciation and security.

Again, masculine protest and resignation—in men as well as women—can reflect in buying behavior. Let us not forget that in this context, "masculine" and "feminine" ways of reacting are not gender-linked. The psyche is neutral.

• Adler (4): The Feeling of Community

Each human being has the capacity for learning to live in harmony with society. Social interest and feeling leaves room for social innovation even through cultural resistance or rebellion. It is rooted in a deep sense of belonging within the stream of social evolution.

As an indivisible whole, the human is also a part of larger wholes—the family, the community, all of humanity, our planet, and the cosmos.

In these contexts, we meet the three important life tasks: occupation, love and sex, and our relationship with other people—all social challenges. Our way of responding to our first social system, the family, may well become the prototype of our worldview and attitude toward life.

The name Adler gave to his system, "Individual Psychology," does not immediately suggest its social foundation. It does not mean a psychology of individuals. On the contrary, Adler's psychology is very much a social psychology in which the individual is seen and understood within his or her social context. Hence, its significance for motivational marketing research.

Following from his view of the human condition, Adler based his psychology on the central concept of *Gemeinschaftsgefühl*, Feeling of Community.

Each human being has the capacity for learning to live in harmony with society. This is an innate potential for social connectedness that has to be consciously developed. Social interest and feeling—another translation of *Gemeinschaftsgefühl*—imply social improvement quite different from conformity. It leaves room for social innovation even through cultural resistance or rebellion. It is rooted in a deep sense of belonging within the stream of social evolution.

The feeling of interconnectedness among people is essential not only for living together in society, but also for the development of each individual person. It has long been well known that human infants who do not have emotional connections with their caregivers will fail to thrive and are likely to die.

All this shows how fundamental Adler's vision of man and the community can be for marketing researchers who know how to make good use of it.

• Adler (5): Happy consumers make a better world

Adlerian psychology offers hope in a time of widespread disillusionment. The revitalization of democracy will have to come from the bottom up, from ordinary people living, loving, and working democratically every day. Why should marketers aim for anything less than reconciling the shopper with the products offered by the free-market consumer society?

Not only marketers are interested in Adler's Individual Psychology. Two political critics, William Greider and Philip Slater, believe that our vision and realization of democracy have deteriorated badly. They agree on one fundamental solution to the revitalization of democracy. The democratic ideal must start within the individual and gradually spread to family, friendships, school, and the field of work.

How does a person develop a democratic character structure or correct an autocratic one? Classical Adlerian psychology provides several practical answers.

First, train parents to develop democratic parenting practices at home that will give children early experience of a democratic family life.

Second, train teachers to develop democratic practices in the classroom. They could extend or correct the home climate.

Universities and businesses are further opportunities for training in democratic living.

Classical Adlerian psychology offers hope in a time of widespread disillusionment. The revitalization of democracy will not only have to come from the top down. It will also have to come from the bottom up—a grassroots movement of ordinary people living, loving, and working democratically every day. Why should psychotherapy aim for anything less, ask William Greider and Philip Slater.

And why should marketers aim for anything less than reconciling the shopper with the products offered by the free-market consumer society in which he or she lives?

• Reich (1): The other, "working class" side of depth psychology

As the depression of the thirties was affecting Europe, psychoanalysis was—and still is—seen as an elitist and expensive affair. People had to be treated with quicker and cheaper methods. Reich wanted to change all that.

Freud, Jung, Adler . . . the great threesome of depth psychology. They have had many followers, particularly in the New World. Nazism, and especially its anti-Semitic and anticommunist components, was responsible for the flight of psychoanalysis to the New World, where it has since developed but not always thrived.

Indeed, as the French psychoanalyst and eminent historian of psychoanalysis Elisabeth Roudinesco points out, the difficult times Freudian psychoanalysis went through and is still going through in Europe have their roots in other problems—political and economic.

This situation, she writes, arises out of the general crisis affecting advanced industrial societies in which man has become a mere commodity. The crisis, at once economic and social, brings with it hopelessness, disillusion, and a questioning of democratic values. Unemployment, reduced incomes, lack of job security and deteriorating working conditions, the rise of corporeal psychotherapies and pharmacological treatments quicker and cheaper than psychoanalysis—all these have contributed to a loss of confidence in the methods introduced by Freud.

Wilhelm Reich, whom the Americans may remember as one of the inspirers of the Beat Generation and the student radicals of the Sixties, had foreseen all that. Although he was a pupil of Freud and a direct collaborator at the first psychoanalytical clinic founded by Freud in Vienna, the political orientation of his writings would cause his rift with the psychoanalytical association.

Since the first psychoanalytical clinic, Reich had widened his practice among the Viennese working classes. There he was confronted with the dreadful conditions in which people lived. Because traditional analysis of patients took a long time—at least one hundred one-hour sessions—and was costly, it was reserved for a limited part of the population that could afford that kind of treatment. Besides, it demanded that the patients have a certain degree of education, which in many cases they lacked.

- Reich (2): Dialectical materialism and
  psychoanalysis for the proletariat

With Freud's initial endorsement, Reich founded a "popular" psychoanalysis. Reich joined the communist party, but soon came into collision with them. After the advent of Hitler, Reich fled to Denmark and later to the United States, where he became a hero of the Beat Generation and student radicals.

As a result, Reich began questioning the social relevance of the prevailing practice of psychoanalysis.

Struck by the social unrest that broke out in Vienna in the middle of 1927, Reich became a member of the *Arbeiterhilfe*, the medical service of the communist party.

With Freud's initial endorsement, Reich will now found a movement for social hygiene, from which grows the *Sozialistische Gesellschaft für Sexualforschung*, which in 1929 opens six centers for sexual hygiene in Vienna. He also begins to write on the relation between dialectical materialism and psychoanalysis: he searches to link the two through the scientific character of the fundamentals of psychoanalysis. In association with the German communist party, Reich founds the *Deutscher Reichsverband für Proletarische Sexualpolitik* in 1931, but soon collides with the psychoanalytical establishment as well as the communist party.

In 1932, the communist youth movement bans his books. After the fire of the Reichstag building in Berlin in 1933, Germany begins tracking down communists. Reich no longer feels secure, settles in Denmark for a time, from where he leaves for the United States in the spring of 1939 to lecture at the *New School for Social Research* in New York, which had offered him the post of Professor of Medical Psychology.

It is from that time on that Reich emphasizes the importance of sexual fulfillment for personal well-being, which made him a hero of the Beat Generation and student radicals with their motto "Make Love, Not War."

Reich argued that sexual success depended partly on orgone energy and constructed so-called orgone boxes to capture it. As he sold them for therapeutic use, the FDA declared them a fraud, but Reich refused to withdraw them. He died in prison while serving a two-year sentence for contempt of court and violation of the Food and Drug Act.

3. A brief history of motivational market research

Or, as they say, you've come a long way, baby

Marketing's scientific roots descend from economics, but (as with economics) putting it on a positivist scientific footing may overstate the case. Effective marketing research attempts to ground its findings in consumer psychology. This is the basis of motivational market research.

• (1): Is marketing a science?

If we want to see marketing as a science, we must first find an answer to some other questions: How do we look at science? What kind of science is marketing anyway? How did the science of marketing come into being?

Some people ask themselves very fundamental questions about marketing. Questions such as: "Where does marketing come from? What is marketing? Where is marketing going?"

Where does marketing come from? Marketing is a branch of economics. A very young branch, which sprouted at the beginning of the 20th century.

Yes, I hear your following question. You did not want to know from which discipline marketing originated, you literally wanted to know where it came from, geographically. I see your lips move: from America, of course. Most other languages do not even have their own word for it.

Were you trying to pretend that marketing is beyond us non-Americans? That we have to go to America, once again, to understand marketing? If you believe that, it means that Americans have done their "marketing of marketing" better than we—and still do.

The definition of marketing is simple. "The activities that aim at bringing goods and services to consumers." Marketing facilitates and stimulates that exchange.

Exchange? As there always have to be two parties involved, each has to have something to offer. Simple? Oh well, recipes always seem simple; baking is quite a different matter—as we shall soon see.

So, marketing is the science of . . . Hold on! Is marketing a science after all?

Whether marketing is a science is a question that marketers prefer to answer with another: Is this question important anyway?

It all depends on how you look at science.

• (2): Marketing, the offspring of economics

Science is the observation, description, experimental research, and theoretical explanation of phenomena. A "phenomenon" is a word we will have to come back to later. Meanwhile: marketing is not an exact science; marketing is applied science.

Is marketing an exact science or is it a social science—in the best sense of the word "social"? Of course, nothing human is strange to marketing, or, saying it with Terence: we are human and let nothing human be alien to us. However, is marketing a science?

One of the definitions of science is: observation, description, the experimental research and theoretical explanation of phenomena.

Please keep those "phenomena" in mind: we will come back to them later. Meanwhile, we can already tell you that many will want to see those phenomena as no more than natural phenomena.

In fact, a synonym of our word science is a definition in itself: learning, knowledge. It is the systematic knowledge of those natural phenomena that makes knowledge into a science, i.e. an exact science. Just like art for art's sake: it is beautiful, but what do you do with it?

From the moment that you *do* something with that knowledge, it is no longer an exact science but an applied science. Applications, however, are always tainted with commerce. Even if it concerns something as noble as medicine. The Hippocratic oath itself alludes to it and warns against it.

Let us turn things around. Generally speaking, marketing is the knowledge we apply to bring goods from the producer to the consumer. Let us be conservative and say that this knowledge is an "applied science." Right. Application of which science? Ah! There you are!

Marketing is a subdiscipline. Yes, there are subdisciplines. Marketing is, or was, a subdiscipline of economics.

• (3): Marketing is more than economics; it is a practice

Marketing is part of economic science or economics. Economics is an exact science . . . as long as you don't do anything practical with it. Marxism, for example, is philosophy rather than economics. Marketing is action.

Economics is a social science, which studies the production, distribution, and consumption of goods and services, and the theory and management of economies or economic systems. Economics is a pure science if you like. You can get pure knowledge from it without doing anything with it. Again, art for art's sake.

And if you want to do something with it? Then marketing can take part in the game. However, is economics a pure science after all?

Yes, Plato and Aristotle have written about economics, but at that time, "economics" meant nothing more than good housekeeping. We are still far from the medieval mercantilism and the Physiocrats of the 18th century; we are still far from Adam Smith and Karl Marx. Actually, both Smith and Marx were philosophers rather than economists.

Of course, philosophy is—more or less—a pure science, in the sense that at the old universities it belonged to the curriculum of sciences and liberal arts, next to law, medicine, and theology. Today, philosophy includes logic, aesthetics, metaphysics, and epistemology. And why not marketing?

Come on, that was only a little joke. The fact is that marketing proves to be difficult to classify. So, should we place it under the heading of economics after all?

When did economics lose its status of philosophy? That was Karl Marx's doing, says Jean-Marie Domenach in his *Enquêtes sur les idées contemporaines.* It was not Marx's only accomplishment. Since Marx, philosophy has also lost its royal standing. Social science explained things about human beings that were more practical than philosophy. Moreover, in our society, it has become more important to act than to philosophize on our existence. It has become more important to change life itself and make life more worth living.

• (4): The offspring of economics has grown up

Economics is a deterministic science that tells sales managers how they should sell and teaches marketing managers how to deal with communication. Communication—and dialogue—is what this is all about: a dialogue with economics and with other sciences, too.

Previously, we mentioned "noble" science, such as medicine. We do not know whether it was his own name that inspired Alfred Nobel to choose physics, chemistry, physiology or medicine, literature, and the promotion of world peace as noble causes to be awarded with prizes. Mind you that economics—in which he himself excelled—was not among them. The Nobel Prize for economics was not awarded before 1969 and then on the initiative of . . . the national bank of Sweden.

Now the incensed heirs of Alfred Nobel want to abolish the "Nobel" prize for economics or at least rename it "prize of the *Riksbank.*" Incensed why? Because economics cannot possibly be counted as one of the noble sciences? Because such a prize is dynamite blowing up the other prizes for noble sciences?

We, too, would be delighted to decouple marketing from economics. It does not mean that we want to blow up our ties with economics. It does not mean that we think the child has outgrown the parent.

Economic science is a sort of commercial science. Economic science has its origins in commerce. Economic science gives us theories and models. It is a deterministic science that tells sales managers how they should sell and teaches marketing managers how to deal with communication.

Communication is precisely what this is all about. If we really want to decouple marketing from that kind of economic science, it does not mean that we refuse to pursue the dialogue. We want a dialogue with economic science—a critical dialogue. We want a dialogue with other sciences, too, with sciences that are hardly ever mentioned in economic science.

The battle between the classical and postmodern views of qualitative market research

We must analyze the meaning of consumption and culture. We must approach consumer behavior in a phenomenological way. We must analyze how goods relate to the identity of the consumer—to the inner world of the consumer—and find out the meaning of this relationship. We must analyze how goods relate to culture—the environment, the outer world of the consumer—and find out the meaning of this relationship.

Here begins the battle between the classical, positivistic view and the postmodern view of qualitative market research.

In classical (positivistic) qualitative market research, they were only interested in the regularity and repetition of certain manifestations. For postmodern qualitative market research, all manifestations are significant. We must research and understand the actual situation as fully as possible.

Classical qualitative market research led to generalities, whereas postmodern qualitative research takes into account particularities and significant details.

Classical qualitative market research dissected. Postmodern qualitative research consolidates to form a whole. That is the whole difference.

Classical (positivistic) qualitative market research is a method that captures reality. It is a method that is based on the discovery and verification of a theory. Classical qualitative market research attaches great importance to internal and external validation, with procedures that lend themselves to (statistical) analysis.

Postmodern qualitative research rejects all those criteria as irrelevant and sets totally new criteria against it.

• (5): The way of existentialism

Marketing is about subjective experiences of the consumer. Some of the underlying processes that help us understand this are shared with psychology and philosophy. The course that we, at Censydiam, followed in philosophy is called phenomenology, popularized as existentialism by Jean-Paul Sartre.

As it is, marketing *is* a dialogue. Marketing is a dialogue between producers and consumers or—as the case may be—between producers and society. In this dialogue, quite a few other sciences are involved. Indeed, this dialogue is not about laws or patterns. It is not even about objective data, but about subjective experiences of the consumer.

In the matter of marketing, it is not the marketing manager who conducts the orchestra. The marketing manager is not a conductor who makes notes in a score sound together in a successful performance of a symphony—that bears his or her self-willed, personal stamp, just like a symphony by Mozart becomes a symphony by Herbert von Karajan. Marketing is more like a work by Béla Bartók.

Béla Bartók collected and systematically analyzed Hungarian and other folk music. Bartók did not indiscriminately adopt this folk music in his compositions, not even as variations on a theme. He did, however, master their scales, melodic contours, and rhythm, and based his own work on them. We immediately recognize this work as Hungarian, but they are no less Bartók. In that sense, his work is related to the works of Zoltán Kodály; they came about thanks to the same underlying processes.

Such underlying processes make marketing, as we see it at Censydiam, into what marketing really is.

One of these underlying processes is shared with psychology and philosophy. Let us talk about the latter.

The course we followed in philosophy is the one that is called phenomenology. No, we do not want to be presumptuous. After all, phenomenology has been popularized by Sartre as existentialism—or was it the other way around, and has existentialism, and phenomenology, popularized Sartre?

Consumer goods, too, have a meaning

This is not about raw material, about "brute" isolated facts that should be tested separately. This is not about testing and validating within the narrow scope of a research theory. This is about human experience in specific situations.

Therefore, we do not use one method or one research theory only; therefore, we use not one methodology, but different disciplines and different research methods.

Therefore, we focus on meaning, on the meaning of consumption, rather than on consumer behavior itself.

Indeed, consumer goods have a meaning. Consumer goods are signifiers *(des signifiants)* and we search for the signified *(le signifié)* and so we end up with another research method—with semiotics, which is a long way away from market research, but can be applied to explain the meaning of consumer goods—and therefore consumption. The French psychoanalyst Jacques Lacan used semiotics to "rewrite" and reconfirm Freudian psychoanalysis.

We must—semiotically—research the meaning of goods because the practical use of things is indissolubly connected with symbolism, with symbolic meaning. It is precisely by these symbolic meanings that the possession and consumption of goods help the consumer (or the user) to socialize, to fit in with society. What is more, they become the signifiers of his or her life.

We must reconstruct the experiences of consumers and interpret the cultural significance of those experiences.

Finally, we must report all this in a "thick" description.

- (6): Is today's marketing a postexistentialism?

Phenomenology is the study of the structures of consciousness that enable consciousness to refer to objects outside consciousness itself. Existentialism, Sartre's form of phenomenology, is a dynamic philosophy. One of the keywords of existentialism is "commitment," which does not mean that we have to commit ourselves, but that we are committed—in the consumer society.

Phenomenology, again, is not a science. But then again . . . Phenomenology studies all possible manifestations within human experience and leaves aside all considerations of objective reality and subjective response.

In other words, phenomenology describes the structures of the experiences such as they arise in consciousness, without appealing to theories, deductions, or assumptions from other disciplines such as the natural sciences. So, phenomenology is the study of the structures of consciousness to the exclusion of all the rest.

More concisely, the founder of phenomenology Edmund Husserl says it as follows: phenomenology is the study of the structures of consciousness that enable consciousness to refer to objects outside itself. What do phenomenologists then find through their studies? What are those structures of consciousness? They are "meanings," in the semiotic . . . meaning of the word. They are "meanings"—for example, the abstract content of perception—that enable us to perform acts related to the objects.

Phenomenology is a philosophy, in the sense of the philosophy that was taught at our ancient universities in the curriculums of science and liberal arts, besides law, medicine, and theology. With one addition: it is a *dynamic* philosophy. Jean-Paul Sartre will drive home the dynamic point of phenomenology. (By the way, the work-shy longhairs that called themselves existentialists had taken hold of the wrong end of the stick.)

One of the keywords of existentialism is "commitment," a word that is often misunderstood. We must not commit ourselves; we are committed (or we do not exist as human beings), and today we are committed in the consumer society or not: we live with it in an open world or we are against it and fight it, such as fundamentalists in their closed worlds.

• (7): The phenomenology of consumption

Phenomenology came as a reaction against positivism that prevailed in marketing for a long time. It is a new view of the world: it gives more attention to the way things show themselves, to what lies hidden underneath ordinary daily experiences and the behavior that results from it.

Marketing as the existentialism of consumption? Is consumption not merely a phenomenological essence? Does it not bear a resemblance to Descartes' *Cogito ergo sum*?

"To think marketing" is not enough. Marketing thinks of something, of certain phenomena outside "pure marketing." One can think in the past, in the present, or in the future, but one thinks always *of something*. Phenomenology rejects the things that exist only in consciousness. We are confronted with things outside our consciousness.

Martin Heidegger, a colleague of Husserl, wanted phenomenology to make known what lies hidden beneath the ordinary daily experiences. Phenomenology came as a reaction against the triumphalist positivism that had prevailed in marketing for a long time. Husserl, and later Sartre, have tried to describe the world before explaining it. Are we, in marketing, doing anything different?

It is a new view of the world, a new view that gives more attention to the way in which things show themselves, that gives more attention to their different aspects.

Why would we do anything else? Phenomenology is a philosophy that is applied to sociology, psychology, to the history of literature and literary criticism.

Psychology is all about making known what lies hidden underneath ordinary daily experiences and the behavior that results from it. Marketing addresses the same questions.

Phenomenology is more than the stereotypic image Sartre and existentialism (often wrongly or not at all understood) have given of it. Phenomenology is a challenge for different schools of thought. A challenge that Censydiam has taken up since its beginning.

• (8): Marketing in search of a scientific model

Marketing is an applied science. As a science, marketing is about constructing and verifying a model. However, a model tells us what happens, not why it happens. In the beginning of marketing, there was the homo economicus, *who consumed. They had forgotten about the* homo emotionalis.

Science is based on research. Marketing is a science. Marketing is the science of consumer psychology. Marketing is based on research—in the broadest sense of the word.

Applied science is all about constructing a model. And verifying that model. Applied science constructs a model that encompasses its subject of research, a model in which all of the facts that were found are fitted. These are deterministic models that have been verified throughout the years.

When clouds are confronted with a cold front, rain falls. That is a fact. Whether it explains the fact is another question. The weather forecaster knows why, but when giving the forecast on television says only that "clouds are approaching the cold front above our region and we can expect rain."

We television viewers are not interested in meteorological (deterministic) models; we only want to know whether or not it will rain. We want to know "what," not "why." We know very well that there are other models. The weather forecaster sometimes even refers to it: "According to other models . . . " We do not ask ourselves "why" the weather will stay dry in other models.

Economics constructs an economic model. Marketing, as a science, evolved out of economics. It is not surprising, then, that when marketing research appeared on the scene of science forty years ago, it worked with models that were seen as "the most scientific" at the time. Marketers first asked "what" and did not feel the need for a model. Research into "why" came only later.

At the beginning, there was the *homo economicus*. This *homo economicus* was a colorless person. He had no feelings, he only performed "economic" acts: he consumed. They had forgotten the *homo emotionalis*. They forgot to ask *why* the *homo economicus* consumed *what*.

• (9): In search of the nose of the homo economicus

How has consumer behavior been explained? First, there was the economic approach, the era of the rational consumer. Then the psychoanalytic approach, the era of the emotional consumer. Then the cognitive approach, the era of the consumer driven by rational decision processes. Finally, the era of the holistic approach, that of the consumer expressing himself by his (consumer) behavior.

Let us give a rough sketch of the development of thoughts about consumer behavior, the development of the science of consumer psychology. Let us give a rough sketch of how we evolved from the economic model to the psychodynamic model. Or, to put it more simply, from the advertising model to consumer psychology.

For some twenty years, market researchers limited themselves to answering the three Ws: what, when, and where. Research was limited to answering some very simple questions: how many and which consumers act in a certain manner? Those were the times of market share, brand recognition, and fidelity. Those were the days when Nielsen stood at the dawn of extensive nose counting.

They did not restrict themselves to counting noses. They also tried to explain consumer behavior. On what did consumers base their choices? Why did consumers react to certain stimuli?

They tried to explain all that by cognitive processes. They tried to read the "black box" between the commercial stimuli and the response—the consumption.

When a plane crashes, there is only one way of interpreting its black box data, and even then the experts sometimes do not agree on the cause of the accident. Deciphering the black box of consumption has been attempted in different ways. No wonder there were different explanations.

There was—obviously—the economic approach. Wasn't marketing a branch of economics? It was the era of the rational consumer. Then there was the psychoanalytic approach, which is older than we would have expected and had been introduced by Ernst Dichter. It was the era of the emotional consumer. There was the cognitive approach, the era of the consumer who was driven by cognitive, rational decision processes. Finally, there was the era of holistic psychology, that of constructive consumers who expressed themselves by their consumer behavior.

• (10): The hidden persuaders on the psychoanalyst's couch

In the fifties and the sixties, Ernst Dichter rediscovered the subconscious. His saying that "people do not always do what they say and do not say what they do" is still relevant today. However, Dichter's ideas soon gave birth to excessive inferences such as those of Vance Packard in his Hidden Persuaders.

All that nose counting and, now and then, also looking into the eyes and sometimes at the hands of the consumer, all those descriptive economic models, told us everything about market shares and their rise, about marginal costs. It told us everything about offer and demand and very little or nothing at all about the consumer.

Then, in the fifties and sixties, they began looking deeper into the eyes and also beyond the hands. Ernst Dichter rediscovered the subconscious. We say "rediscovered" because long before Freud, the 11th-century Arabic scientist and philosopher Avicenna had already discovered the subconscious, but did not do anything with it.

Saying that Ernst Dichter ascribed a symbolic meaning to consumption may be a little bit irreverent. Dichter's legacy is still being transmitted now. His conviction that people do not always do what they say (the cognitive approach) and do not say what they do (and hence that counting noses will not do) is still relevant today.

Ernst Dichter taught us that we could not just ask consumers straightforward questions. We must use other techniques, such as in-depth interviews and projection. These techniques will indeed show us that people do not always do what they say they do and are not always aware of what they do, that their decision-making is not always cognitively determined or inspired.

These are the real values of Dichter's legacy.

In the United States, where the masses often latch overzealously onto new ideas—and drop them soon afterwards—Dichter's legacy has not always been well administered.

"Women bake cakes to give shape to their longing of giving birth to children"? Freud—who admitted that he did not know what women wanted anyway—would not have thought it to be serious. Vance Packard, the author of *Hidden Persuaders*, has written it down in deadly earnest and many were convinced that commercial films were interspersed with subliminal images.

• (11): The comeback of the rational consumer

The excesses of the "psychoanalytic" approach had given marketing, and especially advertising, a bad name. So we went back to models that were more positivistic. Three models will dominate the seventies: the model of the learning process, the social-cognitive model, and the model of high versus low involvement.

It could only be right that after this frightening, Big Brother-like alarm, a new positivist trend found its way into the heads of commonsensical marketing people.

Back to positivism, because the "soft" approach of the—let us call them "psychoanalysts"—had been experienced by many as charlatanism, fraudulent practices, and even a threat. They had given marketing, and especially advertising, a bad name.

This bad name still clings to advertising today, although other reasons are given now. Advertising incites people to buy things they do not need at all. Irrational behavior? So, back to the rational consumer.

Three models will dominate the seventies: the model of the learning process, the social-cognitive model, and the model of high versus low involvement.

The model of the learning process is fairly simple. First there is a cognitive phase in which one gathers knowledge; the very beginning of the learning process. A second phase, which could have been named the emotional phase, but which was referred to more positively—if not positivistically—as the phase in which one built up, or acquired, a positive attitude. Finally, the action phase, action that is in line with that positive attitude.

Socrates and Plato, and maybe even Aristotle, would have agreed with this, as one who knows what is good will do the good thing; one acts according to one's knowledge.

The learning process model was not very remote from the old social-cognitive model that means: behavior as a result of a rational decision, based on information. People learn those cognitive "scenarios" in which they themselves, others, and situations play a role. These scenarios are then applied to new situations because they give the new situations a recognizable meaning.

• (12): Models with exceptions that confirm the rule

The social-cognitive model says that attitudes (based on gathering data) cause intentions, which are turned into action—in our case: consumption. However, not all consumers go through those stages and not in that order. To explain this, a new theory was pushed forward: The Involvement Model.

In 1975, Martin Fishbein and Icek Ajzen developed the Theory of Reasoned Action and the Multi-Attribute Models.

These models—the concepts of the evaluative criteria or attributes—could be presented in almost mathematical formulas: attitude = belief(s) x evaluation(s) of N attributes.

This does not mean much more than that attitudes cause intentions, which are then turned into action; in our case, consumption.

Nice formulas, if you effectively go through all these stages. However, not all consumers go through all the stages of the formula. Some do not go through the stage of extensively gathering data. Some could not care less about conscientious evaluation and just keep buying—or should we use other standard marketing terms, that they buy impulsively or irrationally, unreasonably?

Some others do gather information, but only *after* they have made their purchase, when it is too late . . . to fit them into the beautiful theories of Fishbein and Ajzen. You can't have it both ways: either everyone toes the line of the theory or the theory has too many exceptions to be scientifically founded. Do we want to be scientific or not?

To explain all this, a third theory was pushed forward: The Involvement Model.

The Involvement Model relies on two concepts to explain the differences in consumer behavior: the involvement on the one hand and the instrumental versus the expressive on the other.

As it sounds so convincing, we will go more deeply into it . . .

• (13): Involvement, or emotion against cognition: a heartbreaking choice

Consumers who are highly involved in their purchases will behave differently because they have more knowledge of products and brands and know the differences between the products better. Consumers may also be highly involved not because of the content, but because of the emotional quality of the commercial message.

The Fishbein-Ajzen Involvement Model says, on one hand, that people who are deeply involved ("high involvement" as they call it) process more attributes and apply different rules to make their decisions.

On the other hand, the Involvement Model alleges that with low involvement, affects can form without cognitive processes or behavioral response.

Finally, it appears—according to the same model—that consumers who are highly involved in their purchases will behave differently from the formula above because they have more knowledge of products and brands, because they know the differences between the products better, and/or because they will sooner and more quickly endorse a product.

And the instrumental versus the expressive? That explains the involvement, and even the degree of involvement.

Consumers may be highly involved with a product, not because of the content (e.g. the content of a commercial), but because of the emotional quality: the tone of voice, the style, the personality, and so on.

The value-expressive motive is then set against the utilitarian ("rational") motive. Value here has nothing to do with price or market value, but with meaning, with interest. Here we have affective versus cognitive involvement.

An example will make it clear. When buying a car, one will be more highly involved with the purchase of the car than with the fuel it uses. Yet, both belong to the instrumental field. Cosmetics and cigarettes belong to the expressive field. With which will a consumer be more highly involved? With cosmetics. Right. It is as simple as that.

- (14): First thinking, then feeling, then buying, or first feeling, then buying . . . and so on

These models that combine cognitive models and affective models are doomed to fail in practice. The consumer is not always rational and even with rational consumers we have to consider unconscious, and subconscious, cognitive processes: the time had come for a "new wave" of motivational research.

Let us go through the points once again. Brace yourself and do not forget that we have to keep two axes apart: instrumental versus expressive and high versus low involvement.

Instrumental, high involvement; the process runs as follows: thinking, feeling, acting. Instrumental, low involvement; the process now runs as follows: acting, feeling, and then perhaps also thinking.

Do you remember the car and the fuel it uses? Car: instrumental, high involvement; when purchasing a car you first think, then you feel, and then you buy. When filing up to drive off in the car you just bought, you act first, then you feel, and perhaps you also think.

Where the fuel is concerned it sounds convincing: you fill up, you notice that the car is not running smoothly, and then you think that you might have chosen the wrong octane. Come on, this was only a joke.

Making jokes in marketing, however, can cost you dearly. Especially when you know that when buying a car you first think, then feel, and then buy. When purchasing cosmetics you would (according to the Involvement Model) feel first, then act (that is buy), and then think.

No, we are not telling you another joke, this is serious. We also see that such models—which strive to combine cognitive models and affective models or arrange them according to marketing value and also include impulsive buying—are doomed to fail in actual practice.

During the eighties and the nineties we began to recognize that consumers were not always rational and that, even with those rational consumers, we had to consider unconscious, and subconscious, cognitive processes. The time had come for a second "new wave" of motivational research.

Odyssey 1986 . . . ethnographers on a voyage through the cosmos of consumption

In the summer of 1986, Holbrook, Hirshman, and Belk—it almost sounds like a law firm, but in fact they were a sort of private detectives, private detectives of consumption—set out together and observed ordinary people doing their shopping and consuming products in everyday life.

They may have behaved like private detectives, but their method was not that of Philip Marlowe and even less that of Hercule Poirot. They applied the methods of ethnography.

Indeed, after the "rational consumer" and after the "emotional consumer" and after the "decision-making consumer"—who all exist in a certain way—people felt the need for a "total consumer."

To put it academically: they felt the need for a holistic view of the consumer, the consumer as a total personality who communicated with the outside world by way of self-constructive and self-expressive consumption.

One felt the need for a holistic view in which a situation triggers a set of thoughts and wants that spring from the totality of a person's repertoire.

Those thoughts can be real or unreal (rationalistic or not rationalistic), conscious or unconscious (rational or emotional), and so on. The holistic view includes all previous methods without giving preference to or excluding any.

It is a phenomenological approach of consumer psychology, and of what the consumer consumes, and how. That is the great difference from the previous research methods. We must see consumption as a whole and try to describe the mechanism of that whole—and its structure.

- (15): Dogs do not "talk" with their tails in the same way that cats do

During the eighties and the nineties, the unconscious or subconscious processes were being analyzed in a more rational manner than in the days of Vance Packard. We made a start with the semiotic approach. Market research is indeed interested in the relations between signs and their meanings.

In the preceding decades, it had become clear that unconscious (or subconscious) processes played a part that would not be ignored even in cognitive processes, no matter how rationally the models of those times had been constructed. Precisely because of this, the "new wave" of motivational market research of the eighties and nineties paid more attention to the analysis of unconscious processes, but then in a more . . . rational manner.

The times of Vance Packard belonged to the past and so did his hidden persuaders—which did appeal to the general public, but had not contributed more to motivational research than the Wizard of Oz.

Yes, there were cognitive as well as non-cognitive dimensions in the purchase process, but they had to be approached in a more scientific manner, as a taxonomy of the thought patterns of consumers.

We made a start with the semiotic approach.

Semiotics is a wide-ranging concept that was introduced into philosophy in the 17th century by John Locke. It was later subdivided into three branches: pragmatics—the way in which people use language, semantics—the relation between signs and their meaning in language, and syntax—which relates to signs apart from their meaning.

Market research is interested in the relations between signs and their meanings, in the broadest sense of the word. The meaning of the same sign can differ depending on the user and the circumstances. Tail wagging—a sign—does not have the same meaning for cats, dogs, and horses.

Sounds, too, can have a meaning and sometimes the meaning can transcend different languages. For example, some assume that the sound *i*, as in the French *ici* and the Spanish *allí*, stands for "close to the speaker," whereas the sound *a* stands for "far away from the speaker," as in the French *là-bas* and the Spanish *allá*.

- (16): The consumer acts purposefully,
  but not necessarily emotionally

The structure of cognition can be occasional, can be expressed in words or images, and can also be factual as opposed to procedural, i.e. knowledge that tells us how to do things. All this is taken into account in the new model and allows for both conscious as well as unconscious information processing. Now we must find instruments to measure that structure.

Semiotics is a significant method for analyzing the scenarios that the consumer employs. That is what we want to do: analyze buying scenarios—and this is the new cognitive approach for this analysis.

These scenarios can run on conscious as well as unconscious—or subconscious—cognitive processes. When they are conscious, they are limited and only indicate a direction for solving a problem. When they are unconscious, the scenarios run on automatic pilot; they are, as it were, improvisations.

However, let us first go through the structure of cognition, of the sorts of knowledge.

There is episodic or occasional knowledge. It is tied to a particular time and place. It is the opposite of semantic, general, or conceptual knowledge.

There is the knowledge that can be expressed verbally, as opposed to knowledge that is expressed in images.
Finally, there is categorical (factual) knowledge, as opposed to procedural knowledge, the knowledge that tells us how we should do things: the mental programs.

The new cognitive approach allows for these different forms of knowledge. It explains the behavior of people from an information processing perspective. It allows for both conscious as well as unconscious information processing. It integrates the responses of the emotions as well as of the affects.

This new cognitive approach shows us that the consumer acts purposefully—in a goal-directed fashion—but not necessarily with reason. This means that consumers—and people in general, since all people are consumers—actively (but not necessarily consciously) seek information in their environment and integrate it with existing knowledge to direct their behavior.

Now it only remains to find the instruments to measure this cognitive structure.

- (17): Instruments to measure the level of personality, values, and motivations

The measurements are made on the level of the personality, values, and motivations. On the personality level of the consumer, we inherited two different earlier models: the psychoanalytical approach and the search for motivations in the values. This model looks for the functionality of behavior.

To measure the mental cognitive structure, we must analyze the means-end chains of the mental scenario, the scenario that links the behavior in the outer world with the inner world, the inner life.

The means-end chain runs as follows: first we have the concrete and abstract attributes, then the functional and psychosocial consequences of them, then the instrumental and terminal values, and finally the motivational goals—in a word, motivation.

The measurements are thus made on three levels: on the level of the personality, on the level of the values, and on the level of the motivations.

On the level of the personality of the consumer, we inherited two different earlier models. One one hand, there is the search for the personality of the consumer via the psychoanalytical approach, the psychosocial approach, or the approach of trait theory. Then there is the search that goes the opposite way, namely, the search for motivations in the values, which in turn lead to essential characteristics. This model looks for the functionality of the behavior.

The universal values themselves are presented in this map:

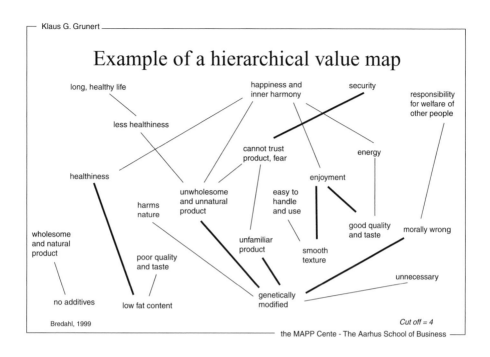

Example of a hierarchical value map

long, healthy life

happiness and inner harmony

security

responsibility for welfare of other people

less healthiness

cannot trust product, fear

energy

healthiness

unwholesome and unnatural product

easy to handle and use

enjoyment

harms nature

good quality and taste

morally wrong

wholesome and natural product

unfamiliar product

smooth texture

poor quality and taste

no additives

low fat content

genetically modified

unnecessary

Bredahl, 1999

Cut off = 4

• (18): A taxonomy of values

Values are beliefs about desirable goals, i.e. motivational concerns that transcend specific situations. Values are the same all over the world, but do not always have the same importance. Here, too, semiotics can help us grasp the real meaning of certain values.

According to Shalom H. Schwartz, who published in the nineties, values are beliefs about desirable end states that transcend specific situations. Values are the expression of a goal or motivational concern, requirements of the human existence to which all individuals must be responsive.

The map of universal values (as shown on the preceding page)[Verify page references in final proof.] makes it possible to classify the fundamental goals with regard to consumer experiences and consumer behavior. They also make it possible to classify a universal structure of values, which are the same all over the world.

"The same all over the world" does not mean, however, that they have the same *importance* all over the world. The sense of honor, for example. Shakespeare's "Brutus is an honorable man" is not the same as the Italian "Onorevole" (a parliamentarian) or "uomo d'onore" (a member of the mafia), or "family honor," which led to a family feud in the mountains of Albania that is still not settled after generations of bloodshed. Here, too, semiotics can help us.

For example, when Palestinian children were presented with sweets after the terror attacks of September 11th, we must know the original context of sweets in their culture. When a Muslim boy is circumcised, his little friends are associated with the event by the crashing of a stone jar full of sweets to the floor. Here the smashing of the jar is a signifier of the pain of circumcision, which is then relieved by the sweets. The sweets themselves are a signifier of the importance of the event. For Palestinian children, sweets carry overtones of many things, including that an important—and not necessarily joyful—event has occurred. This does not give a complete insight into their acts on that day, but it does give more insight into the possible complexity of their motivational framework.

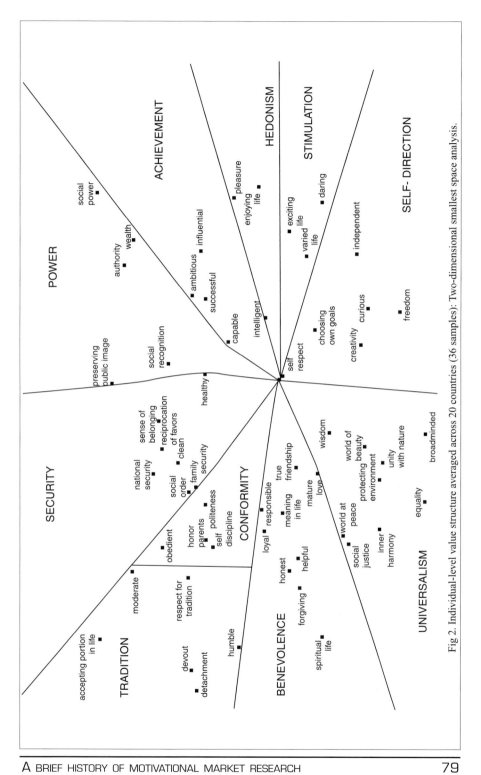

Fig 2. Individual-level value structure averaged across 20 countries (36 samples): Two-dimensional smallest space analysis.

- (19): The universal values that determine the fulfillment of our basic needs

When put in a row, the three basic needs of all humans (biological, social, and the welfare of the group) are translated into motivational goals, which in their turn give rise to numerous values. Therefore, it is logical that those values are universal.

The motivational goals or concerns we just mentioned have their origin in three human survival requirements: the survival requirements as a biological organism, the needs and requisites of social interaction, and the welfare needs of the group.

People have, for example, an organic need for control and mastery. This need expresses itself in the motive of "self-direction," which in turn is expressed (and searched for) in values such as independence, creativity, and so on.

When put in a row, these three basic needs (biological, social, and ecological—ecological in the sense of human ecology, the balance within the social group) are translated into motivational goals. These motivational goals in turn give rise to (or are "filled out" by) numerous values.

Therefore, it is logical that—since humans are always humans—those values are universal and therefore have a universal structure of compatibilities and conflicts, which we can put onto a map as follows:

4. The Censydiam model

Or what we have learned from Plato
and other explorers of the human soul

It is easy to observe and measure the overt rationales consumers use to justify purchases. As with an iceberg, however, the most powerful drivers of consumer satisfaction strategies lie beneath the surface. Censydiam's model yields a powerful tool to harness the insights of depth psychology for effective marketing.

• (1): The submerged part of the iceberg

We can observe attitudes and emotions that are based on logical reason. There are, however, emotions and feelings, urges and needs we cannot so easily observe and are not even aware of. Depth psychology has shown us that our inner world is the real driving force that steers our behavior.

In the course of its development, market research has often told us things that everyone can see: attitudes and emotions everyone can observe, attitudes and emotions that are based on logical reason. These attitudes and emotions inspired product developers and marketers of the past to build certain features and benefits into their products.

There are, however, emotions and feelings that we cannot so easily observe because they are not based on logical reason. There are feelings and emotions, urges and needs that are hidden below the "observable" level, just like the submerged part of an iceberg.

Although icebergs may reach an impressive height of 90 to 150 m (300 to 500 ft) above the ocean's surface, about 90 percent of the iceberg's mass is beneath the surface. Below the waterline, we find the feelings and emotions, the motivations, urges, and needs we cannot see and are not even aware of.

The iceberg may be a good and even literal example of the condition of the human mind, but it does not tell us anything about its function.

Socrates' pupil Plato can help us here. According to Plato, objects in the physical world merely resemble perfect Forms in the ideal world. These perfect Forms are the objects of true knowledge. Everything in the world of space and time, all the things we can observe, is what it is by virtue of its resemblance to its universal Form. The supreme Form is the Form of the Good, which illuminates all other Forms. Knowledge of this Form is the source of guidance in moral decision-making. It is an ideal vision of the world.

Indeed, Plato's theory extends to an individual level, resting on Plato's division of the human soul into three parts: the rational part, the will, and the appetites. The just person is one in whom the rational element, supported by the will, controls the appetite. The small mass of iceberg above the water controls the huge, hidden mass under water? No, we know since then that it is the other way around.

Avicenna—and later Freud, Jung, and Adler—have shown us that the hidden mass of the iceberg, our inner world, is the real driving force that steers our behavior.

• (2): Libido and personality, never-ending causes of conflict

The libido—the psychic and emotional energy associated with instinctual biological drives—often develops into complex and different needs, some of which can become conflicting. Personality, too, can cause conflicts. The question is: How are they formed and can we "measure" them?

Freud's psychoanalytical theory—which we sketched rather comprehensively before—rests on his concept of the libido, among other things. It sits in the submerged part of the iceberg of our psyche.

In its simplest definition, libido is the psychic and emotional energy associated with instinctual biological drives. It is not just sexual desire or the manifestation of the sexual drive, although for Freud it was the energy of the Id or major portion of the unconscious mind, the level of desires. According to the theories of Freud, the libido is indeed the sex *instinct*, which can be rechanneled, or "sublimated," as artistic creation for example. (Carl Jung, however, rejected the sexual basis, believing that it is the general will to live that drives creativity and action.)

If we again refer to Plato, the libido could well be, and often becomes, the worm in the healthy apple produced by Plato's universal Forms. Indeed, the libido often develops into complex and different needs, some of which can be very conflicting. These different needs and the conflicts they cause create a tension that can only be relieved by an adapted satisfaction of the need.

Personality, too, can cause multiple conflicts. We all have unique personalities. But how are they formed?

Behaviorism had its own theories about (almost predictable) personalities. It is the stimulus-response theory in which all complex forms of behavior—such as emotions and habits—are seen as composed of simple muscular and glandular elements that can be observed and measured.

However, Freud believed—and we with him—that unconscious processes direct most of people's behavior. Therein it is driven by the Id, the Ego, and the Superego.

• (3): Personality, or the Id, the Ego, and the Superego in conflict

The conscious and the subconscious are made up of the Id, the Ego, and the Superego, i.e. our desires, our identity, and our morality. They obviously must clash from time to time. These personality conflicts cause a tension that must be relieved. Relief can come from two directions: release from tension or control.

The conscious and unconscious are made up of different levels.

The Id can be equated with the unconscious, which is the reservoir of instinctual drives of the individual. The Id is dominated by the pleasure principle, through which the individual is pressed for immediate gratification of his or her desires. We will call it the level of desires.

The Ego is the central part of the personality structure that deals with reality and is influenced by social forces. The Ego, which begins forming at birth in the first encounters with the external world, learns to modify behavior by mediating between unconscious impulses and acquired social and personal standards. We will call it the level of identity.

The Superego automatically modifies and inhibits those instinctual impulses that tend to produce antisocial actions and thoughts. The Superego develops as the child gradually and unconsciously adopts parental and social values and standards. We shall call it the level of morality.

In these senses, this model of personality corresponds wonderfully well with Plato's division of the human soul into three parts: the rational part, the will, and the appetites. The just person is one in whom the rational element, supported by the will, controls the appetite.

However, we do not live in an ideal world prefigured by Socrates and Plato. There are indeed multiple conflicts between the levels of the psyche. Identity, desires, and morality must obviously clash from time to time.

These personality conflicts, together with the urging libido can cause a terrible stress, an intolerable tension that must be relieved.

• (4): Psychological mechanisms to deal with the conflict

When libido predominates, gratification of desire will be the highest attainment. When conflict predominates, the desire will be suppressed. There are, however, intermediate stages such as sublimation, displacement, regression, fixation, and finally suppression.

Relief can come from two directions, or better, there are two directions relief mechanisms can go: release or control. All depends upon which is the strongest player in the field, the libido or the conflict.

When libido predominates, *gratification* of the desire will be the highest attainment. On the contrary, when the conflict predominates, there is no other way out than to totally suppress the desire.

As always, there are intermediate stages to relieve the stress that is caused by the libido conflicting with the personality. All those stages have their own names in psychology and psychoanalysis, but have become common property. Here you have them, from top to bottom. *Sublimation*, or modifying the natural expression (which is the gratification) in a socially acceptable manner.

Displacement, another defense mechanism in which there is an unconscious shift of the desire from the original object to a more acceptable or immediate substitute.

Regression, the reversion to an earlier or less mature feeling or behavior. *Fixation* is even more immature. It is a strong attachment to a thing, especially such an attachment manifested in immature behavior that persists throughout life. Fixation is persisting in regression. Persons using this strategy tend to cling to it in almost every circumstance.

And finally, *suppression*, the conscious exclusion of unacceptable desires, thoughts, or memories from the mind. In this case, the stress is resolved by flight, pure and simple.

Release

Driven by Libido

gratification
sublimation
displacement
regression
fixation
suppression

Driven by Conflict

Control

- (5): The Self versus the Other, or Alfred Adler completes our model

In his neo-Freudian school of psychoanalysis, Alfred Adler stressed the sense of inferiority as the motivating force in human life. The inferiority complex originates in the Self-image, the conception one has of oneself. The compensation of the complex generates masculine protest (me) versus feminine submission (us).

We have already given a rather detailed sketch of Alfred Adler's theories. As early as 1911, Adler left the "orthodox" psychoanalytic school to found a neo-Freudian school of psychoanalysis. He no longer agreed with Sigmund Freud's emphasis on sexuality, and theorized that neurotic behavior is overcompensation for feelings of inferiority. Adler stressed the sense of inferiority as the motivating force in human life.

Where does that sense of inferiority come from? Contrary to orthodox psychoanalysts, Adler saw Man as more in touch with the outside world. He introduced the Other as an important factor in the function of the psyche.

There is of course the Self, the Freudian Ego. Adler introduced the Self-image, the conception that one has of oneself that includes an assessment of qualities and personal worth. This assessment is defined largely by how we are perceived by the Others.

In Adler's model, Self-image becomes a more important driving force than Freud's libido. It generates masculine protest (me) versus feminine submission (us). You will remember that in Adler's *Individualpsychologie*, masculine protest means the tendency—in men as well as women—to cope with feelings of inferiority in an active way and thereby suppress feminine or feminine-like tendencies. Submission is characterized by constantly expressing a need for appreciation, security, and belonging.

Fundamental drivers of Human Behavior

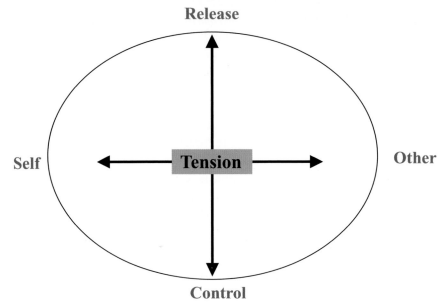

• (6): The map

If we want to provide a clear picture of the strategies that allow people to relieve the stress caused by conflicting need states, we need a map. Here we have it.

8 Basic Consumer Strategies

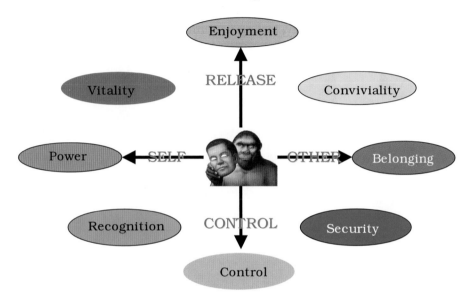

To understand what those strategies really are, we need to define them and see what role they play in behavior, that is, what kinds of behavior correspond with those strategies.

That is what we will do on the next pages. We will illustrate these strategies with images taken from the real world of consumer behavior. We are sure you will not only understand and empathize with these types of behavior because you have felt them around you—and even in you—but also immediately recognize the situations, which are drawn from real life.

• (7): Vitality

Vitality is characterized mainly by achieving independence (away from the Others, as opposed to finding security among the Others). It is achieving individuality by embracing innovation, by exploring new emotions, by an extroverted Self, not in the sense of gregariousness, but exploration of the environment.

Vitality is all about experiencing freedom, passion, adventure, buzzing about, spending energy, feeling very much alive and kicking.

• (8): Power

The Power dimension reflects the need to achieve success and status in life. People striving for the satisfaction of Power want to be respected, praised, and acknowledged for the choices they make. They are situated opposite from those striving to belong and want to climb to unprecedented and solitary heights.

Psychologically, this is all about imitating leadership and acquiring self-esteem through imitative or mirror behavior. In a sense, this is the ape in man.

• (9): Recognition or Status

The Recognition or Status dimension reflects the need to be different, to stand out from the crowd, not drift with the current. Recognition or Status is all about feeling superior—intellectually, culturally, and/or materialistically.

In psychology, Recognition or Status is mostly a compensation for inferiority, for Adler's inferiority complex. People striving for Recognition or Status want their status to be recognized and want to be in control of themselves and of their emotions.

• (10): Control

Sometimes behavior becomes very functional and is triggered by situations and circumstances. When Control is exercised, behavior is void of emotions and feelings.

As psychiatrist Thomas Szasz says, "Addiction, obesity, starvation (anorexia nervosa) are political problems, not psychiatric: each condenses and expresses a contest between the individual and some other person or persons in his environment over the control of the individual's body." The same is true for controlled forms of consumer behavior.

Psychologically, this controlled behavior can be a way to avoid confrontation with (one's own) emotions and passions.

• (11): Security

The security dimension groups the need for comfort, tranquility, and relaxation. Sometimes people need to withdraw, to return emotionally to early childhood experiences, worry-free moments. They want to feel protected, secure, and cared for.

Psychologically, this comes close to what we called regression, but regression need not always be a permanent neurotic state or a reversion to an earlier or less mature pattern of feeling or behavior. Instead, it can be a temporary way out of the stress and the tension.

• (12): Belonging

The need to belong is essential to humans and animals. People need to feel part of a group. People need to feel accepted and supported by their loved ones. They need to feel secure. Belonging is also a need to take care of others, a need for obedience to norms and regulations of the group.

Friedrich Nietzsche saw it as a philosophy of life and its necessities: "What is wanted—whether this is admitted or not—is nothing less than a fundamental remolding, indeed weakening and abolition of the *individual:* one never tires of enumerating and indicating all that is evil and inimical, prodigal, costly, extravagant in the form individual existence has assumed hitherto, one hopes to manage more cheaply, more safely, more equitably, more uniformly if there exist only *large bodies and their members.*"

• (13): Conviviality

Whereas Belonging holds no risks because one withdraws within the group, Conviviality draws one out of one's Self towards the others. As Dick Swiveller says in *The Old Curiosity Shop*: "Fan the sinking flame of hilarity with the wing of friendship; and pass the rosy wine."

Conviviality is the need to open up socially, to really share emotions with others, to have a good time together. It means letting go of social differences. It means having the courage to interact, to take social initiative. It is the need for romance, for intimacy, and for . . . vulnerability.

• (14): Pleasure

In the Pleasure dimension, people try to maximize satisfaction of their physical and emotional needs. No inhibition. No self-control. No social limitation.

Satisfaction is spontaneous and immediate. The purpose of consumption is abundance, enjoyment; it is impulsive and sometimes excessive or even manic.

These extreme forms of Pleasure seeking are rare, because they meet with profound social disapproval. Aristippus, the founder of the school of hedonism, held that Pleasure is the greatest good—which may be true, in theory—and pain the least. He maintained that people should dedicate their lives to the pursuit of Pleasure, but keep dangerous impulses in check. Which dangerous impulses? Disregard for other persons. In a way, hedonism foresaw social disapproval and the Epicureans, or rational hedonists, stressed the virtues of self-control.

- **(15): How to connect the source of needs with the source of satisfaction**

In the womb, we are in the perfect supermarket: all our urges and needs are immediately satisfied. When we come into the world we have to develop successful strategies to reduce the tension between the internal world (the source of our needs) and the external world, in which we can find satisfaction.

When we spoke of the Id, we said that the womb is the perfect supermarket for the baby. In this ideal supermarket, all its wishes—urges and needs—are satisfied immediately. As babies in the womb, we are in a state of total satisfaction: our needs coincide with immediate satisfaction.

When we come into the world, it is a different question: we must develop our own ways of reducing the tension between the internal world—the source of our needs, and the external world—where we can find sources of satisfaction. We must learn to find our way through the labyrinth of the supermarket, we must learn to take our pick from the products that are on offer.

While growing up, we acquire a cumulative set of experiences that lead to satisfaction and gradually we learn to repeat those successful experiences that lead to satisfaction.

The more primary the successful solutions to which people can relate, the stronger the connection between the individual and the solution. All over the world, consumers recognize similar consumption moments and situations that can serve as solutions to satisfy implicit need states.

Behavior = Energy investment which serves to reduce the tension between internal and external world

Need coincides
with satisfaction

.... (birth)

Tension

Source of needs
Internal world

Source of satisfaction
External world

PRENATAL
DEVELOPMENT

INFANT PHASE

CHILD PHASE

ADOLESCENT PHASE

ADULT
• Cumulative set of experiences
  which lead to satisfaction

• The more primary the 'successful'
  solution which you can relate to,
  the more stronger the connection
  between individual and solution

• (16): Satisfaction strategies that will secure a happy solution

The strategies we use will be determined by our personal history. Environmental factors, such as culture, can influence individual choices of satisfaction strategies. However, satisfaction strategies will never be "global"—even if culture becomes more global, they will remain individual.

Behavior is the energy investment that serves to reduce the tension between our internal world and the external world. In this context, we can also call it consumer behavior and we can now fill in our original map with strategies that will secure satisfaction.

"Healthy" persons will use all—or practically all—these strategies at one moment or another. "Healthy" means individuals who have passed through the developmental stages of life, from infant to adult, in a healthy and uninterrupted way. When there is a hesitation, a glitch in this development, the individual will develop a fixation on one or a limited number of need states and limit his or her strategies.

Environmental factors, such as culture, can also influence the relevance of certain need states and individual choices of satisfaction strategies. Social economic development can play its role: productivity growth, improving health, prosperity, expanding education will prompt different strategies. Cultural modernization, with its changing norms, values, and aspirations will influence the choice of satisfaction strategies. The ongoing democratization process, with its freedom of choice, its freedom of participation, and its transparency will broaden the choices and make a more uniform—though not "unique"—world. Satisfaction strategies will never become "global," but remain individual.

We believe in segmentation: the starting point must be
the individual with his needs, not the products.

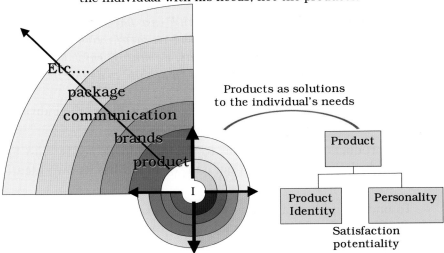

To understand how a product can have a (added) value in an individual's
life one must understand the satisfaction potentiality and the
relational potentiality of a product/brand.

- (17): Let nothing human be alien to us

To understand how a product/brand can have added value for an individual's life, we must understand its satisfaction potentiality. To understand its satisfaction potentiality, we must research how it functions psychologically. We have our very own "machine" to do just that: Illogic.

In the Censydiam model, the starting point is always the individual and his or her needs and desires; not the products.

The products are the solutions to the individual's needs. Just like the individual consumer, a product and/or brand has its own identity, its own personality.

To understand how a product/brand can have value—added value—for an individual's life, we must understand the satisfaction potentiality and the relational potential of that product or brand. We must understand that the satisfaction potential and relational potential must be grafted onto the individual's need state. Packaging, communication, and so on—in a word, marketing—must be based on that need state.

This means that to understand the value of the product in a consumer's life, we must understand how it functions psychologically. To understand that, we deploy a series of research techniques to fathom the psyche of the consumer when confronted with his or her need and with the product that could possibly satisfy it.

Across the world consumers RECOGNIZE consumption moments and situations that can serve as solutions to satisfy implicit need states

**Extroversion of tension
Pleasure
Impulsive**

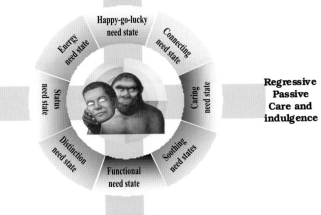

**Progressive
Expressive
Supporting the
identity**

**Regressive
Passive
Care and
indulgence**

**Control tension
Regulated pleasure and use**

• (18): Four different types of brand relationships (1)

Until now, we have always spoken of products, never of brands. Are they the same? Not at all. Consumers have a relationship with a product, but more so with a brand. This relationship with a specific brand is not the same for every single consumer, nor is it the same all over the world. People's relationships with brands are constantly shifting.

Brands are not just names; they speak a language. Brands are the bridges between products and consumers. Brands are the means by which products speak and relate to consumers.

There are four different types of such brand relationships according to how the brand relates with the consumers and vice versa.
When a brand has an absolute, unambiguous symbolic value, we speak of an *absolute brand.*

To be absolute, there has to be a strong social consensus and thus a submissive relationship with the brand, which is expressed in the feeling of "my strong, reliable brand."

As the name itself says, the absolute brand can be relied on beyond all doubt or hesitation. The brand—and the product it represents—stands steady as a rock and has the unfailing confidence of the consumer. It is not a brand to which the consumer entrusts his confidence. Quite the reverse: the brand itself imposes its trustworthiness.

Banks, for example, are—or want to be—such strong and reliable brands. Banks want to radiate an image of absolute trustworthiness. That is why their head offices look like sacrosanct temples, like impregnable fortresses of finance.

• (19): Four different types of brand relationships (2)

When a brand has a strong symbolic value but incites a more mature and critical relationship, we speak of an *adoptive brand*.

Here the relationship is more personal, more differentiating and is expressed in the feeling of "my powerful badge brand."

Again, as the name "adoptive" itself says, the consumer has a quite different relationship with the brand. It is not a brand to which the consumer entrusts his confidence. It is the consumer himself who is confident enough to pin the brand on his own lapel and "adopts" it as his or her own.

There are, for example, many bikers of all sorts. Then there are those bikers who ride a Harley-Davidson. The Harley-Davidson was introduced as early as 1906, when as few as fifty bikes were produced. Ten years later, 18,000 would run along American roads. Today, Harley-Davidson is adopted as a badge brand by "authentic" bikers who want to distinguish themselves from the users of less legendary and newer brands.

On the contrary, when the brand is losing the absolute value that we see in absolute and adoptive brands, when it is liberating and allows explorative experiencing, we speak of a *tentative brand*.

A tentative brand allows that one looks for one's own subjective experience of the brand. It can be expressed as "my kick." The consumers of tentative brands do not submit passively to the brand, nor do they use it as a signboard of their active involvement. They recognize that the value of the brand is very personal and easily accept not sharing this with others.

The language itself tells us exactly what a tentative brand stands for. We say, for example, "I'm on a science fiction kick." It means that one foresees that the kick will not persist. It is the same with some brands that stay on the market only for the short time that tentative consumers get a kick out of them.

• (20): Four different types of brand relationships (3)

Some present-day brands are no longer absolute symbols, but are so fragmented and unstable that they no longer convey authority. Yet, we see consumers enter a mature relationship based on equality. Then we speak of an involving brand.

Here we find a relative, subjective experience, expressed as "my personal brand—for now." The brand no longer stands steady as a rock. The consumer wants to be involved with a brand, but is still searching for how to use the brand as an evenly matched accomplice.

Lately, we are discovering more and more of these brands. They are not brands "for the masses." They offer consumers the possibility of differentiating themselves very personally, often by coming up with a spoof on the brand, like the person who recasted Nike's swoosh into a spermatozoid and wittily remarked: "I just did it". In a word, the "no logo" approach.

This last form of relationship with a brand demands an entirely new look at brands. The BASE telephone company brand clearly does just that. It remains to be seen if they can transform it into long-term relationships, or is this an objective only of the "old brand school"?

Four different types of brand relationships

• Brands have absolute, unambiguous symbolic value • Social consensus about brand • Submissive relationship • **My strong, reliable brand**	• Brands have strong symbolic value • Mature relationship, critical, differentiating • **My powerful, badge brand**
ABSOLUTE	ADOPTIVE
• Brands are losing absolute value • Liberating, explorative experiencing of brands • Looking for own subjective brand experience • **My kick**	• Brands are not absolute symbols, but fragmented, unstable (no respect for brand) • Mature and equal relationship • Relative, subjective experiencing of brands • **My personal brand (for now)**
TENTATIVE	INVOLVING

THE CENSYDIAM MODEL

• (21): Two different types of brand experience

The different appreciations of brands, however, do not always stem from the consumer's own experience of the brand. Sometimes the brand itself imposes the experience, sometimes the experience is self-created by the consumer.

In the case of *imposed brand experience*, the consumer is the passive recipient of a consistent, stable brand image. These brands "speak" only one fundamental truth. This truth, as well as the brand, is objective and fixed. Consumption of such a brand is a normative, receptive act: the brand imposes itself.

In the imposed brand experience, the brand itself commands respect. The significance of the brand has been created and targeted at consumers, not at people. Consumers are not individual people with individual minds, but sort of passive recipients of the forever and always fixed norms the brand imposes.

In the case of *self-created brand experience*, the consumer himself is the active co-creator of a variable and shifting brand image. The self-created brand experience makes room for multiple subjective ideas, for multiple "truths."

In the self-created brand experience, it is the individual who respects the brand, or to put it differently, it is the brand that respects the individual's experience. The significance of the brand has not been created by the owners of the brand but is real in the eyes of the people. We say "people" because in a self-created brand experience there are no longer naked consumers, but real, individual people with their own subjectivity.

Imposed brand experience is all about respect for the brand, whereas self-created brand experience is all about respect for the individual consumer. In the first case, the experience is an experience of the brand; in the latter, the experience is an experience of the self, projected into the brand.

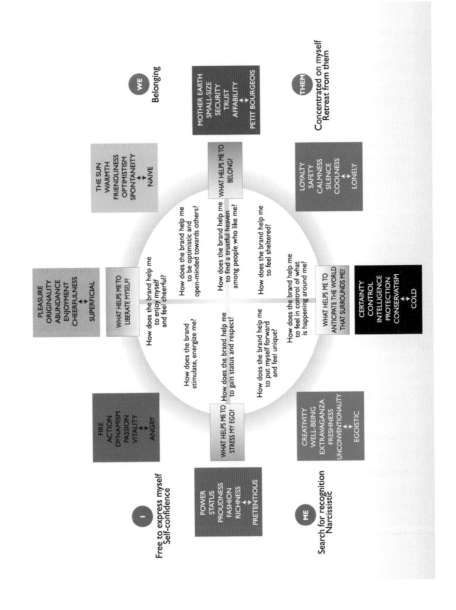

WE
Belonging

MOTHER EARTH
SMALL-SIZE
SECURITY
TRUST
AFFABILITY
↕
PETIT BOURGEOIS

THEM
Concentrated on myself
Retreat from them

THE SUN
WARMTH
FRIENDLINESS
OPTIMISTISM
SPONTANEITY
↕
NAIVE

WHAT HELPS ME TO
BELONG?

LOYALTY
SAFETY
CALMNESS
SILENCE
COOLNESS
↕
LONELY

PLEASURE
ORIGINALITY
ABUNDANCE
ENJOYMENT
CHEERFULNESS
↕
SUPERFICIAL

WHAT HELPS ME TO
LIBERATE MYSELF?

How does the brand help me
to enjoy myself
and feel cheerful?

How does the brand help me
to be optimistic and
open-minded towards others?

How does the brand help me
to find a trustful heaven
among people who like me!

How does the brand help me
to feel sheltered?

How does the brand
stimulate, energize me?

How does the brand help me
to gain status and respect?

How does the brand help me
to feel in control of what
is happening around me?

WHAT HELPS ME TO
ANTICIPATE THE WORLD
THAT SURROUNDS ME?

CERTAINTY
CONTROL
INTELLIGENCE
PROTECTION
CONSERVATISM
↕
COLD

How does the brand help me
to put myself forward
and feel unique?

FIRE
ACTION
DYNAMISM
PASSION
VITALITY
↕
ANGRY

WHAT HELPS ME TO
STRESS MY EGO?

CREATIVITY
WELL-BEING
EXTRAVAGANZA
FRESHNESS
UNCONVENTIONALITY
↕
EGOISTIC

I
Free to express myself
Self-confidence

POWER
STATUS
PROUDNESS
FASHION
RICHNESS
↕
PRETENTIOUS

ME
Search for recognition
Narcissistic

5. Conscious and unconscious

Or reason versus emotion and
imaginary versus the symbolic

The psychology of motives is critical to understanding consumer
behavior. In a sense, this necessitates understanding the underpinnings
of consumer imagination. The power of imagination consists not only
of the power to make a representation based on a few impressions; it
also consists of a world already constructed, based on the one that
interprets these impressions. Marketing often communicates with
symbols. A symbol can also call up reality. It does so, however, by
means of a sometimes arbitrary code. How each consumer's
imagination deals with these symbols is affected by his or her specific
culture.

• (1): Reason versus emotion, conscious versus unconscious

The power of imagination consists not only of the power to make a representation based on a few impressions, it also consists of a world already constructed, based on the one that interprets these impressions. Just like the imaginary, a symbol calls up reality. However, it does so by way of a sometimes arbitrary code.

We have seen at length how psychoanalysts have explored Man's conscious and unconscious. We have seen how they gave emotions a distinct place in the psyche. Jung has pointed at the importance of symbols and archetypes. Yet, what can we do with all of this in marketing research?

Consumers are more than their reason (or intelligence) alone. Man often behaves illogically and thus irrationally. When a respondent tells us that a concept is satisfying because it is logical—producers propose many logical *reasons* such as healthy, less fat, functional, etc.—it does not tell us much about the respondent's behavior. Does he or she feel happy (*emotion*) with this purchase?

When it comes to emotions, market researchers are often rather vague, content as long as their concepts contain emotion. In fact, emotion means that the internal balance (the balance of all incoming or internal stimuli) changes and shifts. Yet there are many emotions we can describe: being happy, sad, guilty, scared, moved . . .

When we conduct research, it is important not only to find out whether a concept triggers an emotion, but to know what kind of emotion it is and whether the emotion leads to desired behavior. Motives give interpretations to emotions. That is why the *psychology of motives* is so important and why we devote so much space to it.

Intelligence and emotion do not entirely coincide with conscious and unconscious, though they often go together. When we think and act logically, we often do so consciously, whereas we are often unconscious of our emotions. Yet there are conscious and unconscious emotions. One can be conscious of one's manifestations of anger or, on the contrary, unconscious of one's inner anger. By becoming conscious, an emotion is not rationalized. Nevertheless, one can recognize the irrationality of one's emotion.

• (2): The imaginary versus the symbolic

When we are researching, we must not only find out whether a concept triggers an emotion; we must know what kind of emotion it is—and whether this emotion leads to the desired behavior. Motives give an interpretation to emotions. That is why the psychology of motives is so important.

The distinction between the imaginary and the symbolic is even more difficult to explain.

Imagination belongs to Man's power of inventiveness. We could say that Man reproduces, or copies, the world of his inner self. All stimuli that enter it are integrated in that world. Therefore, the power of imagination consists not only of the power to make a representation based on a few impressions, but also of a world already constructed, based on the one that interprets those impressions. That is why the imaginary is also an important reservoir of every individual's cultural identity. This cultural identity sits in the way of what we call globalization, which we will discuss in the following chapters.

The imaginary also has a gestalt quality. Gestalts are the specific applications of the theory of imagination. For the viewer, images break into gestalts because they are interpreted in their imaginary world. The stereotypes are already there and changing a small detail is enough for another stereotype to be applied.

Gestalt effects are typical of the imaginary. People interpret a concept in its totality. A detail can lead the meaning of the totality into a very different direction. The practical consequence is that research into concepts must always begin with questioning the total image.

So it is clear what the imaginary is, but what is the symbolic? Just like the imaginary, a symbol calls up reality. However, it does so by way of a code. Thus, we can speak of a symbol when the connection between a stimulus and its meaning becomes arbitrary.

One might think that the sound of brand names would be unimportant since they are symbols having nothing to do with the meaning they call up. Yet this is not true. In addition to their purely symbolic meaning, sounds also have an imaginary meaning, which is called up by the tone, by the color of the sound. The symbolic meaning of the sound is also strongly influenced by culture, including the language people speak. The imaginary meaning, on the other hand, is universal.

6. The psychology of motives

Or why a motive is much more
than just a reason why

Product managers and marketers fail when they operate without a well-structured psychological understanding of consumer motivations. Every person has his or her own theory concerning why human beings think and act as they do. This theory is generally based on personal experience, but there is a global pattern of how consumers attempt to satisfy their needs. Effective marketers need to be aware of this pattern.

• (1): The need for a coherent frame of reference

Every person has his own theory on why human beings think and act. It is based on personal experience. Indeed, every human being has a self-image and will interpret behavior of others in a way that matches one's self-image and cannot conceive a homogenous structure.

To understand the function of motives, we need to understand their scientific frame of reference, the psychology of motives.

The question of why human beings act is a difficult one to answer. Various answers have been given through the ages. All those answers are reflected in the various systems of psychology.

Almost every person has his or her own theory on why human beings think and act. All human beings—even the least complicated ones—act on and think of their own behavior and the behavior of others based on an implicit theory.

This may be an unscientific psychological system, rarely made explicit, but it is no less efficient. It is a fact that this very personal psychology is inevitably built on personal experience and therefore very subjectively colored. The environment in which one grows up plays a decisive role here.

Lacking a broad and well-structured psychological theory, supported by insight, product managers and marketers fall back too spontaneously on their personal psychology. This is the risk that marketing policy takes when product managers are repeatedly replaced. Each individual has his or her own "personal" psychology that differs from that of others, and all continuity and homogenous structure is lost.

It is clear then what makes the study of human motives so difficult: human beings have self-images. They observe and analyze their own motives. This observation is far from objective. They want their self-image to be consistent, internally as well as in time. Therefore, they will interpret their behavior in a way that matches their self-image.

Motivational research, reviled for twenty years and then restored to honor

All that science, all those theories, all those models . . . all very well, you say, but what are we doing with it in actual practice? How do we interpret all this and how will we apply it to actual market research?

You want to call it research? Very well. We shall call it research.

In the sixties and the seventies, motivational research, which we inherited from Ernst Dichter, took a severe blow.

There was a tendency towards extremism. Extremism of the antirational view, of too great an interest in post-rationalism.

There was social criticism on exposing forbidden needs and desires—that were not quite "politically correct"—and what was even less politically correct: the notorious "hidden persuader" and other subliminal tricks.
There was scientific criticism of using clinical/psychological—not to say psychoanalytic or psychiatric—methods such as projection techniques and so on.

It was said that all these things were not relevant as far as market research was concerned and, even worse, in the matter of marketing. It was said that all these things did not count anymore when they were extended to large groups of the population.

In short, it all worked perfectly as long as it was done in private—in the "lab" of the motivational researcher—but did not go further.

Ten, twenty years later—in the eighties and nineties—there was a renewed interest in the analysis of the subconscious mind, or at least in understanding non-cognitive aspects of consumption.

They did, however, devise a new name for it: The Consumption Experience. After the miscarriage of post-rationalism, postmodern consumer research was born.

• (2): The self-image is not a motive

The self-image has given birth to different theories—the cognitive dissonance theory, "the foot in the door effect," or the initiation effect, and so on—but we must not forget that people pretending to proceed from their self-image do not talk of their real motives.

Beautiful theories have been constructed to support this: self-consciousness, information processing theories, and so on.

One of these theories is cognitive dissonance. When asking people on the verge of buying a car to evaluate it, the evaluation will be much higher than after they have bought it. This shows that the reasons consumers give as motivation for having bought a product are not the real motives; they crop up after they have acted in order to match the act with the self-image. This subsequent justification is the basis of the rationalizations that plague market researchers.

Another theory fitting the same pattern has the name of a selling technique: "the foot in the door effect." Once you have persuaded the consumer to put in a little effort, he or she will be even more prepared to make a greater effort still. Once the route is taken, it is easy to continue: "First borrow a book from a neighbor, then borrow his car."

This is also based on self-image: one who makes an effort incorporates it into his or her self-image. "I'm kindly disposed towards my neighbor. See, I lend him a book!" This is also called the initiation effect. Closed communities often impose trying initiation rites. These trials strengthen the loyalty of the members.

This effect also strengthens product loyalty. In these cases, it is very important to strengthen the consumer's self-image. Striving for congruity is not a motive in itself. It can, however, be an important mechanism to take into account.

When people pretend to operate from their self-image, they do not talk of their real motives. A mother pretending to buy a product because it is healthy for her baby may be doing so out of a need for control. Another mother pretending the same thing may in fact indicate that she projects the concern for her own health onto her baby.

• (3): Ideals and social desirability

Ideals are best described by three conditions: first, an ideal is supported by something an individual lacks; second, there must be a similarity between the ideal and how people see themselves; finally, ideals are supported by people and do not come out of thin air.

Every self-image contains a certain measure of aspiration, of ideals that mobilize individuals as well as the group. One identifies with a group because one shares the group's ideals.

What is an ideal? There is no simple answer to this question. We tend to compare ideals with social desirability. An ideal is what is proper, or better: an ideal is what is proper to be ideal.

Inevitably, we arrive at common descriptions: having everything, health, tranquility, a family . . . Although this is the answer most respondents give, it simply cannot be true that these are the ideals of the majority of people. Still, these "ideals" continue to be used in commercials.

In reality, ideals are best described by three conditions. First, an ideal is always supported by something the individual lacks, by a shortcoming. Second, it is necessary to have a considerable similarity between the ideal image and the way in which people see themselves. In fact, that is why the ideal image and the self-image are so close to each other. Finally, ideals are obviously supported by people and do not hang in the air as abstract notions do. Abstract ideals do not move us; the concrete images of the powerful, of the rich, of the caring mother do.

This could lead us to the conclusion that ideals are always connected with seeing, with the images one can form. This is not completely untrue and it explains why television is such a powerful medium. It would be more correct, however, to say that ideals belong to the register of the imaginary. Ideals belong to the powers of the imagination and the eye is the privileged instrument of the imaginary.

People find each other on the basis of ideals. In other words, they find each other more often for what they do not have but would like to have than for what they actually have. The current lifestyle categories—when they work—are more often a compilation of ideals than an actual lifestyle with which the consumer can identify.

• (4): And if Pavlov's dog became anorexic?

Motives are not the same as needs. Consumer behavior is not an acquired answer to needs. Consumers are guided by a complex web of stimuli. However, the consumer is saturated with (commercial) stimuli and has activated a defense shield. Breaking through this shield is the marketer's greatest challenge.

Is a motivation the same as a need? Do people act on the basis of needs? Is that the explanatory factor?

An answer has been given by behavioral psychology. Behavioral psychology established needs as the key to behavior.

Need presumes necessity and we need certain things to survive, as do rats, the behaviorists' main objects of study. Eating, drinking, sex, and shelter are primary needs for the preservation of the individual and of the species. The behaviorists' discovery consisted of the fact that each of these needs could be used as a system of rewards in order to learn behavior. Everyone knows how Pavlov trained a dog to salivate at the sound of a buzzer. It was indeed sufficient to repeat the signal in combination with food to "teach" the dog to salivate upon hearing the alarm.

We want to discourage marketers from comparing consumers with rats and dogs and regarding their behavior as acquired answers to needs.

It is a fact that consumers are guided by a complex web of stimuli. Mastering this complex web of stimuli—at the level of the shelf, or in advertising—is certainly the future marketer's greatest challenge. The consumer is saturated with stimuli and has long since activated a defense shield. It is no longer easy or cheap to break through this shield. In fact, global marketing is looking for the global Pavlovian buzzer. The question is whether the global buzzer exists.

Everyone knows the mysterious disorder called anorexia nervosa. It is a psychic disorder for which, until this day, no organic origin could be found. Anorexia nervosa makes a mockery of the theory of needs: where do we stand now with our idea that food is a primary need? It becomes even more interesting when we listen to what people with anorexia think of food. We see a total inversion of the theory of needs. While we would expect food to be the object of a need, we see here that "no food" has become the object.

• (5): The origin of motives, the mother motive

Human motives are not the same as needs; they arise from needs. Our first needs are recognized by our mothers. For a mother, a child's cries can have many meanings and therefore she will react in a non-systematic way; the child will develop a range of meanings. A cry for food becomes more than a cry for food. This extension from food to warmth, security, and so on, gives birth to a motive.

Human motives arise from needs. When a child is born, it comes from a state without needs into a state with a myriad of needs. The human child is born as a little animal and, what is more, as the most helpless of animals. The environment determines whether it will develop as a human being or as an animal. It is the mother that makes the difference.

Mother and child must rely on communication to understand each other's needs. Among animals, communication is instinctual; human mothers have largely lost this ability.

For a human mother, a child's cries can have many meanings. It may be thirsty; it may have wet itself; it may want to be cuddled . . . The mother's desire determines what meaning she will give to the cries of her child. Therefore, she will react in a non-systematic way.

Through these non-systematic reactions, the child develops a complete range of meanings. For Pavlov's dog it had been simple: "buzzer" meant "meat" and that was that. For the human child, things are completely different: the expression of its hungry feeling gets different reactions. Hence, it is self-evident that "food" becomes more than merely "food": it becomes charged with a whole range of meanings such as warmth, mother, safety, security, and so on.

In the same way that the mother assumes the child also cries when it wants to be cuddled because it misses its mother, the child develops the meaning that food is more than food alone, that it is motherly warmth, motherly care and love.

The expansion of the meaning of food to warmth, safety, and security gives birth to a motive.

The motive is thus born from the mother.

- (6): Motives. A connotes B, and C, and D . . .

Motives are a web of vague connotations, qualifying the way in which human beings organize their lives. A motive is like a motif, a pattern, steering one's behavior according to the vague design of the motif. As human motives, unlike animal instinct, are not unidirectional, they can be very dissimilar according to the individual.

At this point, we must specify how we define "motive." We must not see the motive in the narrow sense of a rationale, a "reason why." Only if we understand it as a "motif" may we get a truly operational definition. Such a motif, a pattern, can be compared with the designs of carpets and textiles: motifs that are regularly repeated.

Such a motif/motive is the representation of all connotations that go together for one person. It is not, however, a fixed association such as: A means B. This would be too simplistic. For human beings, it means a loose association: A connotes B, and C, and D . . . It is a sort of vague impression of connotations, qualifying the way in which a human being organizes its life.

Does the motive then have the significance of a rationale? It does, a little. One moves within the motive, steering one's behavior according to the vague design of the motif. This definition may sound imprecise, yet it gives a workable solution for the complex subject that motives indeed are.

Ultimately, we are not interested in the real, philosophically true motivations of human behavior. What we want to do is understand something about the two characteristics of human behavior, which are truly relevant for us: the specificity of human behavior and its diversity that, as we see when we compare it to the animal world, can be very distinct and very dissimilar according to the individual.

We could give different names to the motive that was born: the motive of security, of warmth, of being all cuddled up . . . However, let us keep the mother motive as a working title. We shall see later that it will prove to be very workable.

This definition of the motive also enables us to understand how the same motive can be fitted with different meanings in different cultures, with different individuals, with different products.

Eventually, it is not more than a vague connection of meanings, allowing different signs to be selected to represent the motive.

• (7): The mother motive versus the father motive

The mother motive is feeling the need to retreat, to feel secure—it stands for passivity. The father motive is the outside pole, which makes us want to go out and discover the world—it stands for activity. This is true in every society: every child has to deal not only with its inner emotional life, but also with the feelings of other human beings in relation with itself.

The mother motive may be the first motive that originates in the evolution of the human child, but it certainly is not the only one. Being the object of care, being unassuming, feeling warm and secure, also has its disadvantages.

Though one can say that every human being feels the need to retreat from time to time, to feel secure, it is also true that he or she is inquisitive. A child also wants to go out and discover the external world, to dominate the world in an active way.

This is the second motive—and we could call it the father motive. Within the family, two parental functions are always present: that of the mother and that of the father. More often than not, the father stands for the outside pole: he is the representative of the outside world, of conquest and mastery over the external world.

Both father and mother motives play their part in human behavior. It may be difficult for you, the reader, to believe that both father and mother motives play their part in every human undertaking, in all human behavior and, accordingly, in everything concerning commercial processes.

Anthropologist Margaret Mead pointed out that this phenomenon appears in every society. In every society, the child has to deal not only with changes occurring in its own emotional life, but also with the changing feelings of other human beings, especially its parents, in relation with itself.

Every movie, every novel, is marked by mother and father motives. Of course, it is only visible when we treat the motive in the broad, maybe even vague sense we gave it. This means that not every movie or book deals with mothers and fathers. Yet, the elements of activity versus passivity, of man against woman, always play their roles and every plot—whether in a movie or a novel—is based on the conflict between those two aspects.

• (8): Mother and father, the double face of pleasure

There is yet another dimension: that of pleasure. One could say that the first dimension—the father versus mother motives—corresponds with the dimension of active versus passive pleasure. The problem in our developing cultures is how to regulate pleasure, i.e. the need for allowing pleasure and the need to control it.

The distinction between motherly and fatherly aspects of motives does not tell the whole story; it does not map the entirety of human civilization. One could say that every mother and every father always has two faces.

Motherliness can have a pleasant, cheerful, warm, and sociable face, but also the face of reticence, pomposity, and even of oppression. While fatherliness can have the face of strength, action, domination, and capability, it can also present a side that does not want to have anything to do with his family, who simply sits around.

With what do those different faces correspond? Why such differences? There must be another dimension we have not yet discussed. This dimension deals with pleasure, but so did the first dimension. One could say that the first dimension—motherliness versus fatherliness— corresponds with the dimension of passive versus active pleasure: passively undergoing pleasure versus actively seeking it. This again corresponds with the feminine and masculine ways of enjoyment. This does not mean, however, that these forms of pleasure are solely reserved for women and/or men: they are enclosed in cultural motives.

This seems to be a very stable pattern: even though our society is on its way to breaking through these fixed roles, we see how the differences of masculinity/femininity and activity/passivity always come back.

The second dimension also deals with pleasure. To human beings, oddly enough, pleasure always seems to be problematic. With human beings, pleasure has been freed from its fixed ties with instinct. This is also why humankind progresses, why humans do more than is strictly necessary for their survival or the survival of the species.

On the other hand, when nature (instinct) does not regulate pleasure, humans have to take over. However, humans always have problems with self-regulation. This creates a great need for allowing pleasure and also controlling it; and that is exactly the distinction to which the two faces of mother and father correspond.

• (9): Are we all dissatisfied psychopaths at heart?

According to psychoanalysis, ordinary behavior and psychopathological behavior do not show real differences but are merely positions along a continuum. Psychopathological behavior expresses discontent: the desire can never be satisfied; the person wants to persist desiring, wants to remain dissatisfied forever.

Psychopathological behavior clearly proves that people have problems with their own pleasure. Psychopathological behavior must indeed be understood as a curtailment of pleasure.

The fact that people have problems with pleasure would actually prove that no one can claim to be free from psychopathological behavior since the measure in which it occurs and disrupts one's balance marks the distinction between actual disturbance and normal behavior.

It is also interesting to look at psychopathology because exaggerated forms of behavior can be studied much more easily than restrained and inconspicuous behavior such as . . . consumer behavior! Moreover, psychopathological behavior has been the subject of more intensive study.

Ordinary behavior and psychopathological behavior do not show real differences but are merely points along a continuum. According to psychoanalysis, psychopathological and normal behaviors have their places in a continuum.

Psychopathological behavior can be roughly divided into two categories: hysteria and obsessive-compulsive neurosis.

Let us look at hysteria. It is very difficult to give a definition of hysteria or of behavior that can be labeled hysteric. One could say that hysteria has to do with discontentment, with structural dissatisfaction regarding the fulfillment of needs. Hysteria is characterized by a desire that cannot be satisfied, by discontent. One is never satisfied and one does not want to be satisfied.

So, what is hysterical behavior? In the stricter sense, this behavior expresses discontent. However, there is something fundamental hiding beneath this, namely that this person can never be satisfied on the level of desire. In other words: this person wants to persist with desiring, wants to remain dissatisfied forever.

• (10): Hysteria, showing oneself off to get an identity

When interviewing consumers, hysteria can distort the results of a qualitative study. Although hysteria—pertaining to the mother motive—can take the form of exteriorization or showing-off, it remains fundamentally a passive motive precisely because it is a reaction against the mother motive itself. It is a rejection of passivity that is always combined with a lack of identity.

It is certainly true that hysterical behavior—either physical as symptoms in the body or social in the sense of giving everybody a hard time—always expresses discontent.

One also sees that hysteria fits within the mother motive, precisely because it is the mother who gives everything and at the same time covers everything up. In fact, it is the hysterical mother's most fundamental complaint that all she has given never seemed to be enough.

One comes across hysteria in market research when interviewing consumers. It is a deceptive phenomenon, which can distort the results. When doing qualitative research, one suggests solutions. Whether one will get a hysterical reaction depends upon the person who conducts the individual interview or group session as well as the way in which one proposes these solutions.

The hysterical reaction can be of the kind expressed by: "What you are offering me is altogether insufficient." The more solutions are presented as ideal, ultimate solutions, and the more the respondent suspects that the chairperson of the panel backs that solution, the more intense the reaction will be.

We can also find it in different segments in which hysteria represents the pole of exteriorization, of showing off. A hysterical segment, for example, can be found in matters of clothing, furniture, and so on, but also of travel and slimming products. They are always characterized by a fundamental need to show off, to distinguish oneself from others.

Nevertheless, we have to see it as pertaining to the mother motive or the passive motive, precisely because it is a reaction against it. It is a rejection of passivity that is always combined with a lack of identity. It is very difficult to assume an identity when taking a passive stand and merely undergoing pleasure.

• (11): A sublimated form of pleasure, a double-edged sword

We could say that the refined, polished pleasure such as enclosed in many products corresponds with the father motive, in a sublimated form that is. On the other hand, we can say that on the motherly side pleasure is enclosed in a generosity and cordiality that found its sublimated form in something that is excessive, smothering.

In one respect, there is the unconstrained pleasure, the pleasure that is allowed, that one can freely experience. At the same time, there is also within the same figure, within the same motive, the pleasure that has to be regulated, that has to be restrained. In each case, there is the pleasure that has to be adapted, that has to be sublimated, if it is to be allowed.

Thus we could say that the refined, polished pleasure—such as enclosed in many products—is a sublimated form of the very expressive, vital pleasure that is enclosed, for example, in brute muscular strength or in some sports that one is allowed to enjoy freely. Alternatively, one could say that on the motherly side pleasure is enclosed in the generosity, in the cordiality which finds its controlled or sublimated form in something that is strong, excessive, overpowering, and sometimes also oppressive. It is a double-edged sword.

Research into very dissimilar subjects repeatedly shows the same patterns and the same motives. Every consumer seems to have his or her own blueprint according to which he or she can satisfy desires. When we superimpose the behavior of various consumers in various situations and in various cultures, we always find the same global pattern.

This does not mean that this is a static global pattern that could be copied indiscriminately from one object of research to another. As with the motives, its loose and therefore dynamic associations of meanings characterize this pattern. If we want to map the singularity of the motivations that are relevant to the subject concerned, we must introduce, in each subject of research, fundamental specifications and nuances into this global pattern.

7. Cross-culturally correct marketing

Or does globalization exist in marketing and is there a "global" consumer?

Understanding human motivations is critical to success in marketing. The mechanisms of the human soul are universal, but because humans have different life stories, they also have different motivations. To discover motivations is the reason why we do motivational market research. Marketers have to understand motivations across cultures because they need to communicate with those motivations across different cultural contexts in order to be successful. There is no such thing as a homogenized, global consumer, despite the fact that psychological models can be universal.

• (1): Standing out and fitting in

The mechanisms of the human soul are universal, but as humans have different life stories, they also have different motivations. To find out motivations is why we do motivational research. We have to do this across cultures because we need to communicate with those motivations across different cultural contexts.

Why should one embark upon cross-cultural research, cross-cultural motivational research that is? Don't human beings' motivations correspond with the same needs all over the world? Can "souls" be different? Of course not. The mechanisms of the human soul are universal. A homemaker in suburban Chicago may well have the same needs and motivations as a woman of the Namibian bush. At the same time, this same person might have motivations that are quite different from those of her immediate neighbor: it all depends upon her personal history. To determine this is why we do motivational research after all.

As we said before, one's personal history indeed may be—or certainly is—shaped by the culture in which one lives. One will find that there is more similarity between the motivational patterns of homemakers in Chicago or between those of women in the Namibian bush than between these distant cousins. However, when it comes to cross-cultural research, this is not the most important point. The most important—the crucial—point is that we, our products, our brands, *need to communicate* with these needs and motivations and *need to do so in different cultural contexts.*

In marketing—and notably in "global," or worldwide marketing—standing out is not nearly enough. In global marketing, you also want your product or brand to "fit" in with the culture of your clients.

But, many will object: why on earth would that be a problem? We have learned everything about multiculturalism . . .

• (2): Multiculturalism, the dream that became a nightmare

Global communication will not bring about the kind of multiculturalism so many optimists have hoped for. On the contrary. These new contacts between cultures have made people more aware of the values of their own cultures and even make them question some of our—western—values.

Multiculturalism is the dream of many societies, especially those who owe a great deal of their economic—and cultural—strength to immigration from all over the world, like New York did at the beginning of last century. In his controversial book, *The Clash of Civilizations*, however, Samuel P. Huntington posits that the beautiful dream of multiculturalism will not only fail, but turn into a nightmare.

More mobility and unlimited means of global communication will not bring about the homogeneous multiculturalism hoped for by so many optimists. The new contacts that are now possible between different cultures have only made "the rest of the world" more aware of the values of their own cultures and even question some of ours.

We must not forget that—despite global communication—some non-Westerners do not adopt or share or even try to understand our view of life. They see it as arrogant and imperialistic, while others embrace it for reasons that would be foreign to Westerners. We all remember the Third World's outcry against "Yankee imperialism." We waved it aside and thought it would all soon disappear, together with the autocratic regimes that belched that sort of propaganda. They are still there, and new ones have joined them.

Marketers cannot work on a multicultural basis and make the same mistakes politicians have made and are still making. If there is a war to be waged—not against terrorism but rather to conquer new markets—we marketers want to win that war.

The strategy can only be cross-cultural. In these waters, marketers should not thrash like overpowering sharks and make disturbing waves, but swim gently like a fish.

In global marketing, the question is not how to stand out in a different culture; it is how to stand out while fitting in. Standing out in a different culture—without at the same time fitting in or blending in—is to be singled out. And to be left unsold on the shelves.

• (3): Culture, a discussion on the Internet

Politics, religion, and language are all elements of culture, but culture is much more than that. People who practice the same religion do not necessarily have every cultural trait in common. What, then, are those elements that are more relevant than political ideology, religion, or language?

What exactly is "culture?" A few years ago, Elie Dib Wardini of the Institute of East European and Oriental Studies at the University of Oslo launched an interesting discussion on the Internet. Wardini was disturbed by the polarization that is happening—East versus West, North versus South, Islam versus Christianity, et cetera—and the tendency to see culture as monolithic—our culture, their culture, and so on.

Wardini proposed his own view on Culture, which he insists on writing with a capital C. "In referring to Middle Eastern Cultures, writers and speakers often allude to the Arab, Persian, Turkish, etc. Cultures," Wardini posted. "What do these terms mean? What do they imply? Are these the true cultural boundaries in the Middle East? It is the opinion of the present writer that the use of these terms is often faulty and misleading."

"The problem with the use of the terms 'Persian Culture,' 'Arab Culture,' 'Turkish Culture,' etc., in my opinion, arises when it is assumed that political ideology, religion, or language forms the basis for definitions and generalizations concerning 'Culture.' Of course, politics, religion, and language are elements of culture, but Culture is much more subtle and complex. There are innumerable elements that combine to form a people's Culture and sub-Cultures."

"It would be wrong," Wardini explains, "to assume that certain cultural traits are necessarily common to people who are bound by a political ideology, a religion or a language, just as it is wrong to assume that people having many cultural traits in common also have a common language or political ideology. Worse yet is when one projects modern ideologies and concepts back in time, 'creating history' based on modern 'realities'."

What, then, are those other elements that are more relevant than political ideology, religion, or language? Wardini speaks of elements that contribute to the formation of "cultural clusters," a term borrowed from the linguistic "Sprachbund." Wardini uses "cultural clusters" to denote a group of people who live in geographically adjacent areas and who share a large amount of cultural traits, yet do not necessarily form a single ethnic group.

• (4): Culture, a question of values?

Values are more important elements that bind people "of a same culture" together across the boundaries that are drawn by language, religion, or ideologies. Take the example of the values of the extended family, or of time, which is money for us but not for everyone.

We do not know if anyone ever pursued Wardini's proposal to further discuss "Culture." We could not find traces of it on the Internet. It might well be that Wardini gave too many answers already. However, did no one speak of "values?"

Let us go to a culture that is completely different from ours and find out whether "values" are an integral part of culture. Important values for Indonesian women are marriage and having children. The orientation is more toward the extended family than to the nuclear family we know in our western culture. (The value of the extended family is, of course, not exclusive to the Indonesian or Muslim "cultural clusters.")

The extended family orientation allows average Indonesians to stay with their parents much longer than their counterparts in the West. Many Indonesians stay with their parents even though they have a job and even after they have married.

The family becomes the center and the basis of numerous activities: traveling, vacationing, eating out, monthly shopping, and so forth, are usually extended-family affairs. The family thus becomes a means of social control and the most important reference group for its members. Quite a few marketers took the hint. Shining examples are Indonesia's best-selling cars: family vehicles, which seat more than six passengers. The communication tactics of one of these brands clearly targeted the extended family, in the broadest sense of the word. It said this car is good because it is for the whole family: mother, father, sister, brother, granny, uncle, and auntie . . .

Another Indonesian example: time. Although the saying "time is money" is known all over the world and is also used in Indonesia, Indonesians do not really see time as having a price. They are perfectly willing to work after office hours without being paid overtime, but on the other hand it is difficult for them to understand the real meaning of a deadline or to be on time at a pre-scheduled meeting. Indonesian local time is "jam karat" or "rubber time."

• (5): Censydiam swims like a fish in cross-cultural waters

Every human being is unique, yet we can also detect similarities, as we all have basic needs. However, as soon as we start talking about extras in life, (cultural) differences between people emerge. As long as you respect the fact that people differ from yourself but also from other people in the same global consumers' group, you will get to the true essence of the consumer.

At Censydiam, we take our cue from the idea that consumers are first of all human beings. To address the consumer correctly, you have to address the human being. Obviously, each man and each woman is unique; each individual stands for him or herself. Yet we can also detect a number of similarities, e.g. we all need food, drink, housing, and clothing. As far as these basic needs are concerned, we are all the same. Once we start talking about the extras in life, however, difference between people emerge.

Apropos of cultural differences, does this imply that we cannot research women and men who belong to a culture that is different from our own? This would also mean that male researchers would not be able to talk to young mothers, or that female researchers could not possibly interview young men about a subject such as football.

We believe that you will get to the true essence of the consumer as long as you approach your consumer as a person, as *a whole human being*, and respect the fact that people differ from yourself and *also from other people in the same global consumers' group* (e.g. mothers in one cultural group using disposable diapers while in another they will prefer cloth).

For example, when we talk to mothers to find out what kind of diapers they will prefer, we first spend quite some time discussing how it feels to be a mother. We can only connect the reason for using either disposable or cloth diapers to a particular mother if we know how that woman sees herself and her role as a mother.

When we apply this to consumers in a specific cultural environment, we must also find out how they actually experience the fact of belonging to that particular culture. This empathy can only exist when your researchers have a clear insight into that specific cultural environment or—even better—belong to it themselves. Only then can they move like a fish in cross-cultural waters.

• (6): Advertising seen as an element of culture

Different cultures perceive commercial communication—or advertising—in different ways. This often causes a gap between the sales argument and the reality of the product. Sometimes nothing is wrong with the product but everything goes wrong with the communication.

The differences in the perception of communication—or advertising—are also an important element of culture. In Europe, it seems that the British find commercials fun, but that the Germans and the Spaniards reject them. So do the Russians, while the French—quite philosophically as one might expect from the French—adopt a more lenient and conciliatory view. All this should make advertisers think.

The reason is obviously not economic, but cultural. There is no reason why the rich Germans and the poor Russians should both dislike commercials.

The British, merchants at heart, accept without being shocked that manufacturers exalt the virtues of their goods. Besides, British TV commercials are funny; they are highly creative and amusing to watch. The Germans, on the other hand, do not see why TV commercials should be funny—or creative. They want to know everything about the product, and this is exactly what they get: didactic and even pedantic commercials that cannot possibly make them "dream."

Is this what causes the gap between the sales argument and the reality of the product? Why do advertisers refuse to make the Germans dream? Are Germans really nothing more than "gründlich," or thorough? Cross-cultural research could also show marketers that there is more to German "Kultur" than what made a certain German leader of the past immediately draw his pistol.

Almost 90% of the French think that advertising makes people buy "things they do not need." It may well be that those people do not "need" those products, but they certainly do . . . "want" them.

If an advertising campaign makes people feel guilty about buying the product, there is probably nothing wrong with the product, but everything is most certainly wrong with the communication!

- (7): *The Clash of Civilizations* and pan-Arabic research

After the attacks on the Twin Towers in New York, our views of the Arabic world have changed. Has the Arab world itself changed since we discovered it in the 19th century? Not in all its aspects. Censydiam researches Arab society "globally"—i.e. as a whole, with all its different components.

Samuel P. Huntington's famous book, *The Clash of Civilizations* (which has become more famous still since September 11th) has prompted us to dwell on a culture that is so often misunderstood: the Arab culture.

Does our motivational research have anything in particular to say about Arab society? Is there a difference between the Arabs and the rest of the world, as Huntington wants us to believe? Moreover, why do we say "Arabs" and not "Muslims" or "Muslim society"? If it is true that religion can strongly determine a particular culture or society, it is certainly the case with Arab culture and society.

Why does Censydiam use the term "pan-Arabic research" anyway? Do we use it in the political sense of the word? Certainly not. We use the term "pan"-Arabic in the same sense that we use the term "global" when we talk about "global man": we want to research Arabic society as a whole, with all its components including religious, ethnic—or geographical—and cultural.

In the 19th century, we "Westerners," formed a picture of "the East," of the Near East in fact. The French called it "the Orient." Egypt and the Holy Land were at its center. It was a cultural interest: the Orient of the Orientalists—the Orient of the painters and the writers. Its impact was strongest in France and Britain, but for different reasons.
When Napoleon invaded Egypt, he did so less for military or political goals than for cultural reasons. Bonaparte was accompanied by a retinue of scientists, archeologists, architects, painters, and poets who were to describe Egypt in a sumptuous forty-volume *Description de l'Égypte*.
Conversely, the British interest was concentrated on the Holy Land and on spiritual values, which had nothing to do with Islam for that matter. It was the Holy Land of Jesus and nothing else. The Arabs, although picturesque for the painters, were seen as nothing but troublemakers for the politicians.

• (8): Europe and the Islamic world

Europe has a long history of contacts and even association with the Arab world. Today, we see a strong wave of immigration of Muslims in almost every European country and Europeans have learnt to live with a "soft," tolerant Islam although there are unfortunate exceptions on both sides.

In this century, the interest of the West in the Near East is no longer cultural but political.

It all began with Thomas Edward Lawrence, "Lawrence of Arabia," whose political interest led to a sociocultural empathy with the Arab people. The term "Arabian" took on a totally different meaning, best described in Lawrence's magnum opus *The Seven Pillars of Wisdom*.

Over the past few decades we have developed a different picture of the Near East. The "Arabian" characteristic has given way to "Islamic." Moreover, there still is a difference between the European awareness and that of America. It has historical reasons.

On one hand, different European countries have had colonies and mandates in Muslim countries. France in North Africa—which boasts two of the major holy cities of Islam, Fez and Kairouan; in Syria; and in Lebanon, with its French-inspired intelligentsia. Great Britain has had mandates over Egypt and Palestine. Since 1799, the Netherlands has had direct control of the East Indies—which was to become Indonesia—where Islam has been the dominant religion since the 16th century.

On the other hand, we see a strong wave of immigration of Muslims into almost every European country, even those that had no experience of Muslim culture in the past, such as the Scandinavian countries, Italy, and Germany with its important proportion of Turkish workers. A second and third generation of Muslims is born in these host countries.

In her colonies and mandates as well as with her immigrants, Europe has always been living with an open, tolerant, and "soft" Islam. Europe has even seen a very particular and distinguished example of it in Spain. In 711 AD, Muslim Berbers invaded Spain from North Africa. The Moors, as the Muslim invaders were known, soon conquered almost the whole peninsula. Under the Moors, Spanish cities, industry, and agriculture prospered. Great centers of Moorish culture were Toledo, Granada, and Seville, where Muslims, Jews, and Christians worked together in harmony and understanding. The Muslim thinker Averroës held that philosophic truth should be derived from reason rather than from faith, an opinion that is sadly lacking in Muslim society today.

• (9): The United States and the Arab world, a different story

For different historical reasons, the United States has experienced Islam and the Arab world in a much more unfavorable way. As several Arab countries have since been branded of aiding and abetting actual or psychological terrorism, the distinction between Arab culture, religion, and nations has become confused.

The result of all this ancient and more recent history of living with Islam is that Europe today is more open to Islam than the United States.
The United States first experienced Islam when leading Afro-American activists began embracing Islam in protest of segregation and domination by white society. Americans suddenly had to deal with a militant and even intolerant ideology such as Malcolm X and the Nation of Islam represented.

Then the real bombshell exploded. If the American people still had any doubt about the nature of 20th-century Islam, many made up their minds on November 4, 1979, when American hostages were taken at the embassy in Tehran. Taking hostages (or launching terrorist attacks) is not really what Islam teaches—and the apologetic hostage takers have made that perfectly clear since—but it was the kind of Islam that took hold in the American collective unconsciousness.

Ironically, "Islamic" and "Arabic" have become confused in many American minds since then, though Iran is not exactly an Arab country; Iranians, or Persians, are of Indo-European origin. It was this Islam however, and this "Arab" world, that made it possible for Samuel P. Huntington to write an essay that could never have been written in Europe. Even the extreme nationalist parties in Europe are more reserved when they speak of the "Arab threat."

To top all that, there were the terrorist attacks of September 11th. For many in America, terrorism became synonymous with Islam and vice versa. It seemed that Huntington's prophecy had already come true and that the next Great War would not be one between nations but between cultures. As several Arab or Muslim countries have been branded with aiding and abetting this kind of terrorism, the distinction between culture, religion, and nation becomes even more confused.

CROSS-CULTURALLY CORRECT MARKETING

• (10): Islamic social consent versus western democracy

Freedom and democracy are the greatest values in our western society. Seen from this angle, "Islamic" could be seen as "undemocratic." Is it really true that all Arabs are hostile to democratic ideals? Motivational research can shed light on all these preconceptions, and help us understand the real cultural differences that in the end help drive consumer decisions.

We saw that Samuel P. Huntington's *The Clash of Civilizations* brought us an interesting message. It predicts the next world war not as a war between traditional political and economical superpowers and not even as a war of ideologies, but as a war between cultures. Moreover, according to Huntington, the greatest threat would come from the fringes of the Muslim world—which actually seems to have become true.

Still, this has nothing to do with the specific domain of religion. It has everything to do with values and institutions. "The western world has to recognize that the peoples of other cultures have not accepted our western values and institutions," says Huntington. "The West must realize that its values and institutions are unique but not universal. Non-Westerners experience the western world as arrogant."

What are the values that set the standards of our culture and our institutions? Freedom and democracy, to be sure. In the eyes of the western world, Islam is not only a religion but also an ideology and a cultural entity. Which is true. A small step hence from claiming that the Arab world is essentially undemocratic. Seen from this standpoint, "Islamic" is no longer opposed to "western values"; it is opposed to "democratic."

However, can we truly call a society and all its people intrinsically "antidemocratic"? There may well be a consensus among the citizens about the fact that divine law precedes the law of the people. But perhaps it could also be that the actual aggressive attitude of the western world towards Islam—which dates back to the Crusades—is pushing the Islamic world in general and the Arab world in particular to affirm their own identities and reject not only the western nations' policy, but their culture, too. Lack of understanding can build on itself, building ever greater misperceptions. Painting any culture with too broad a brush is always dangerous.

Motivational research can diagnose all those preconceptions, biases, and false interpretations of culture and religion. It is especially important

---

where it concerns the Arab world and its civilization—as different from ours as it is. Indeed, the Arab world may have a calling to play an important role in the near future, though perhaps not exactly the role that Huntington foretells. What can we do but hope that he is wrong?

• (11): The Arabs and their "soul"

Can we fathom the Arab unconscious? Is the concept of unconscious not a typically western notion? The Arab scientist and philosopher Avicenna "discovered" the unconscious, "the hidden energy of the soul," in the 11th century, long before we did in the West. Psychoanalysis is now being reintroduced into Palestine. Is the Arab world westernizing after all?

From a motivational marketing perspective, we do not want to repeat what others have stated about the Arabs. We want to understand and interpret the Arabs' deepest longings. To do so, we want to fathom their unconscious. But then again, is the concept of the unconscious not a typically western notion? A Moroccan psychoanalyst maintained that his patients did not have an unconscious. A typically Arab witticism? An "arabesque" so to speak?

We have already seen that the unconscious, "the hidden energy of the soul," was discovered by none other than Ibn Sina, or Avicenna, in the 11th century and its functioning was described in his summa of medicine.

Nevertheless, in the modern Arab world there is indeed a certain reserve against psychoanalytic therapy. However, is it not the same reserve Christian churches in the West have always shown? In a rare interview, French psychoanalyst and historian of psychoanalysis Elisabeth Roudinesco pointed out that psychoanalysis could only exist in a society that meets two conditions.

"The first is the existence, over a long period, of a constitutional state in the form of a constitutional monarchy or a democracy as we know it. A state that protects minorities, allows freedom of thinking, of association, and freedom of the individual in his/her expression. The second is the institution of a psychiatry worthy of its name, which pulls insanity away from the domain of the sacred and the magical."

Roudinesco adds, "That is the reason why psychoanalysis is, for example, absent from the Islamic states." It is perhaps an unfair statement, considering that Sigmund Freud himself had to flee his homeland, which persecuted a minority that at the same time often thrived in the midst of Islamic society. The face of history can quickly change; not that of time-honored culture.

It may be true that Avicenna did not suggest "healing" insanity through "depth psychology." However, it is also true today that it is not uncommon for Arab children to undergo psychotherapy. Just so, motivational market research is effective even in cultures that may be somewhat hostile to depth psychology.

• (12): The future of the Arab world

The Arab world has one face turned toward the values of the past, another turned toward the future, which will not necessarily do away with those values but integrate them. It is a future that will draw its force from both traditional Arab and modern western cultures, from traditional values and from intellectual openness and curiosity, which certainly exist in the Arab world.

The image of the Arab—or Muslim—world, as it appears from the results of our own psychodynamic motivational research, has two faces.

One face is turned toward the values of the past, the other resolutely turned toward the future, a future that will not necessarily be westernized. The turmoil and upheavals within the Arab world are largely due to the difficult and trying search for a new equilibrium and stability.

We must also be aware of the fact that Arab society at present has developed two different cultural communities. There are the nomadic tribes, such as the "authentic" Arabs of the Empty Quarter or Arabia Felix, and the rural communities, the farmers. We are not talking here about the Bedouin or the Egyptian fellaheen. We are talking about their culture, which found its way into the new urban centers of Saudi Arabia and the Gulf States and, respectively, in the big cities of North Africa, Egypt, and the Middle East.

Here lies the future of the Arab world. It is a future that soon will draw its force from values of both cultures, from traditional values—many of which the West regrettably has lost—and from intellectual openness and curiosity, which certainly exist, no matter what Elisabeth Roudinesco and Samuel P. Huntington may say.

The fact that young female college students in many Arab countries are—of their own will—now adopting the veil that their mothers rejected is not necessarily a contradiction or return to the past. It may well be a sign that they—and their fellow male students for that matter—want to be the motors of a new Arabian culture that will readjust the balance of traditional values and modern needs.

We see these phenomena not only in the Middle East, but also in Turkey—an Islamic country that wants to be a member of the European Union—and among the third-generation Muslims in Europe.

- (13): Cross-culturally correct or "global"?

Does a "global consumer" exist or is he on the rise? If he existed, we would not need psychology as a basis for a "global" approach. The problem is that the advocates of the "global consumer" tend to mistake commercial "codes" for "culture."

There is a tempting marketing theory stemming from the idea that a "global consumer" could exist, global in the sense of "worldwide and homogeneous" and not in the sense of the "complete" consumer as we see it. This theory is, of course, also quite different from what we call "cross-culturally correct" marketing.

If a "global consumer" existed, we would not need psychology as a basis for a "global" approach. It would not be the marketer's job to globalize market information; the consumers themselves would behave in a uniform way in different places all over the world.

Those who believe in the existence of a global consumer identify him as the Americanized cosmopolitan. The "global consumer" would be a new breed that began its career in the sixties, the last evolutionary step that reached the highest rung of the ladder that *homo sapiens* could ever reach.

Via television, the "global consumer" feeds on American culture, replacing the ideals of his own cultural community with those of the American Dream. He shares this ideal with countless other Americanized world citizens. Advocates of this school of thought pretend that this type of consumer is on the rise. Recent history shows that this is not at all true. Advocates of the "global consumer" tend to mistake "codes" for "culture."

A good example of that code is the "Marlboro man." The problem is that, in this particular case, the code is mistaken for the message. What appeals to the consumer is not the code itself, but the meaning it generates and the promise it expresses.

The entire world knows the Marlboro man—and the cowboy for that matter—but what is a cowboy to a camel-riding desert-dweller? Does he prefer to smoke a different brand that displays another code, the dromedary?

• (14): The hamburger, culture and/or psychology

There will be no more "global culture" than there will be "global consumers." The histories of different cultures are the histories of psychological behavioral mechanisms assimilated generation after generation, to be able to deal with fundamental human problems. These mechanisms differ in every culture.

When referring to a "cultural approach," we are not saying that the world is on its way to blending into a single, uniform culture. Just like psychology, culture theories attempting to define the differences between cultures have the ambition to globalize. Understanding and describing cultures implies that you attempt to study large groups of people globally. There are no major contradictions between psychological and cultural marketing theories. Cultural theories ultimately do appeal to psychology to find an explanation of behavior.

In Europe, for example, third-generation immigrant children tend to be enraptured with American culture. Among other things, they fancy hamburger restaurants. Americanization? Careful observation tells us a different story. For American youngsters, the hamburger has the meaning of "not belonging to the original family." For the parents, that is why the family restaurant is a powerful motive for making their children "digest" their independence. For European youngsters, this motive has been toned down to an effort to become independent: the hamburger is a sign of belonging to a peer group.

For some immigrants' children, however, the hamburger has a different meaning. Being crushed between two cultures—the culture of their parents and the culture of the country in which they are growing up—they reach for a third culture that will enable them to get out of the dilemma.

The histories of cultures are the histories of psychological behavioral mechanisms assimilated again and again, generation after generation, so as to be able to deal with fundamental human problems. The difference between Catholic and Protestant cultures is an example of such a cultural approach in search of psychological interpretative mechanisms. Our next story will give some examples of this.

A psychological explanation makes it possible not only to interpret cultural differences from a single point of view, but also to see the interrelationships of the different elements of a culture.

• (15): How to "globalize" Protestants and Catholics

An example of how long before the commercial world thought of "global marketing," religions applied their principles by addressing people across the cultural individualities with basic solution strategies.

Attempts to globalize sometimes come up against the walls of religious differences. However, they manifest themselves in consumer patterns that have nothing to do with religion itself.

A consumer with a strong Protestant background often has a need for control. He wants to control his own and his children's behavior. It explains his needs for rules, for portioning, for portioned and re-sealable packing: a Protestant does not want to commit the sin of squandering or at least needs the impression that sinning can be avoided.

In Catholic culture, we will observe a different attitude. Here, sin is a fact, as it were. Sinning is part of living. We are speaking here about trifles such as candy, chocolate, and fatty food. In Catholic culture, there is a more prominent need for penance: one can redeem these peccadilloes. Hence, the massive need for rationalization and arguments that can justify "sinning."

"Money does not smell" is a saying that suits Protestants better than Catholics. In Protestant culture, formalization—which money in fact is—is fully accepted. Formalization strips object of their substance, maintaining only their form. This principle can be observed in religion itself: no images of God, no substance, a totally abstract faith. God, religion, and money are quite different things.

Catholic culture formalizes guilt, and money is an object signifying guilt. Instead of formalizing guilt—the pleasure that money buys makes one feel guilty—instead of stripping it from all of its substance, Catholic culture brings it to the forefront: one cannot have pleasure if one does not at the same time feel guilty. For Catholics, money definitely smells. In a sense, long before the commercial world thought of "global marketing," religions applied its principles by addressing people across cultural individualities with basic solution strategies.

Christophe Fauconnier and Jan Pollaerts

8. The Censydiam Illogic Algorithm

Or more thoughts about our vision of man
and how we created an instrument to decipher
consumer text

Motivational market research is extremely challenging to conduct, but Censydiam's Illogic Algorithm is a unique tool that helps harness its complexity for our clients in a timely manner. The Censydiam Illogic Algorithm is a computer program for interpretive analysis of consumer statements (gathered as text during interviews) and finding motivational clusters. It is based on our structural model of the underlying dimensions of consumer motivation.

• (1): Combining two approaches of qualitative analysis

The Censydiam Illogic Algorithm is a computer program for the interpretive analysis of consumer text and finding out motivational clusters. It is based on our structural model of the underlying dimensions of consumer motivation.

The Censydiam Illogic Algorithm—Illogic for short—is a computer-assisted methodology for interpreting qualitative consumer data, based on a theory of behavioral functionalism. This software combines the merits of two approaches in qualitative analysis.

The first is interpretative analysis with its focus on careful and sensitive understanding of the subjective significance of *consumer text.* We will develop understanding from data upwards, using—as in grounded theory—the interplay between data, coding, and display.

The second approach is the theory of needs and, more recently, the taxonomy of values, where an underlying universal structural frame of "motivational clusters" is being confirmed. The Illogic software will indeed find its organizational codes in a structural model of the underlying dimensions of consumer motivation (the Censydiam model), but will use them as intuitive categories in a process of exploration of the meaning of consumer behavior (the Illogic software).

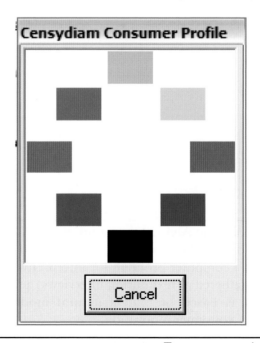

- (2): We need to understand consumer behavior as an "answer" to underlying needs

We have to distinguish overt behavior from the underlying need-tension it intends to solve or at least diminish. In other words, we need to understand consumers' thoughts, emotions, and activities as behaviors aiming at producing effects that "answer" the underlying needs.

Consumption implies a wholeness of predispositions to behave in a particular way, to appreciate the same objects of consumption. The concept of behavioral functionalism states that all consumptive behavior—with certain stability in space and time and in a particular context for a particular person—must be understood as functional toward underlying needs. The focus of analysis should not be the behavior itself, but the effect it has on a consumer's need state.

We have to distinguish overt behavior from the underlying need-tension it is intended to solve or at least diminish. From the perspective of the individual consumer, this need-functionality is exactly the "meaning" he or she gives to behavior. Thus, understanding consumer behavior requires a very accurate and detailed description of the subjective "meaning" of the behavior, an understanding of the individual experience of the effects of that behavior.

We need to understand consumers' thoughts, emotions, and activities as behaviors aimed at producing effects that "answer" the underlying needs.

So, what are these needs towards which behavior is functional?

In literature on needs and motivation we can distinguish two major orientations.

One is the need-theory approach where, in consecutive articles, new needs and classifications of needs are presented for measurement and testing. Need itself is defined as a personality variable characterizing a personal tendency to behave in a certain way.

The other orientation is the view of needs as a subjective process of creating chains of gratification, memories of experience of links between behavior and psychological consequences.

The strong internal logic of Illogic

The use of intuitive categories as organizational codes enables us to introduce new tracks of logical and illogical analysis; by means of speculative ideas, we can form new hypotheses, test them, and double-check them.

Illogic forces the analyst/researcher to think and empathize with the data that have been gathered and give them need-relevance. It forces him or her to interpret every part of the data (the "field text") in the light of the underlying mechanisms of need-satisfaction.

The researcher/analyst must understand the subjective experiences of the respondent, the release, the sublimation, the repression, and displacement of energy.

Illogic is a tactical machine that generates "meaning" in the text, but in doing so it respects the richness of the text itself and at every moment allows the writer of the report to go back to the original, rough and virgin text whenever necessary.

Illogic enables the researcher/analyst to gain insight and a better understanding while staying very close to the factual text.

- (3): Need as a personality variable and as an interpretation

Studies repeatedly affirmed the claim that ten distinct motivational value types are recognized across cultures. They form a system of higher-order value clusters that are set out on the same motivational continuum. Illogic gives a visual representation of those value clusters.

There is a growing literature identifying different new needs in which needs are defined as a personality variable. Researchers study the effect of need states on, for instance, attitude change and information processing. However interesting this approach may be, it does not seem very relevant in trying to explain particular behavior in a consumer context since it does not lend itself to exploration, only to verification.

Another development in need theory presents the concept of "personal values" as the expression (and measurement) of the goals that motivate people and of their perception of appropriate ways to attain these goals. Some disagree on the universal content and structure of these values. They propose that the primary content of a value is the type of goal—or motivational concern—that it expresses. These goals or concerns represent three universal requirements of human existence: needs one has as a biological individual, needs one has as being a member of a group, needs of the group itself. According to Shalom H. Schwartz, whom we mentioned earlier (see "A taxonomy of values"), from these primal needs a specific number of distinct motivational types would be derived.

Cross-cultural replication studies repeatedly examined and affirmed the claim that ten distinct motivational value types are recognized across cultures and that they form a system of higher-order value clusters that are arrayed on the same motivational continuum.

The interesting notion behind this approach is not the listing of yet another set of needs or values, but the concept of a universal need structure.

In consumer research, laddering techniques and means/end value mappings are used as measurement and visual representation of the links between—concrete and abstract—product attributes, functional and psychosocial consequences, instrumental and terminal values, and finally motivational goals.

From fieldwork to field text

Postmodern qualitative research is not based on counting noses and not even on interviews alone. Postmodern qualitative research is also based on ethnographic literature. How can we otherwise tell a client how to position a product in the Muslim world after the attacks of September 11th? Modern ethnology deals not only with distant peoples in dark continents: there is an ethnology of the populations of the suburbs, the high-rise apartment buildings and tenements—an ethnology we cannot possibly learn from interviews and random sample surveys alone.

Postmodern qualitative research is also based on historic accounts, on the news that tells us more about how the inner world of people behaves as opposed to the outer world. The reaction of people to the news and the manner in which the media bring us certain stories teaches us more—or something else—than our interviews.

If we want to know how people react to fast-food restaurants, we can go there and observe them, but we should also know the story of that political activist who dismantled such a restaurant at the head of a congenial gang. In fact, the same man—and the same group of people—caused riots during the world trade conferences: not the sort of people we will interview in the thick of battle, not the sort of people that before or after the riots will tell the same story as the media . . .

The life history of a leader, who for the rest has nothing to do with the client's product, can show us how someone at the top (just like the product) efficiently reacts to successes and misfortunes.

Then there are, of course, the personal interviews and the personal experiences of the interviewer himself.

All that gives us text. Text we have to work on, text we have to interpret, facts that we shall examine through phenomenology, statements that we must decipher by means of semiotics.

• (4): From "motifs" to motives

In determining a person's needs, it is more relevant to study the complex patterns or "motifs" of connotations between a person's inner world and all the objects and other persons in the outer world surrounding him.

From a purely methodological perspective, "grounded theory" argues that theory should be generated and developed through interplay with data collected in actual research. Especially in the study of human behavior, grounded theory stresses the researchers' responsibility for the interpretation of what has been observed, heard, or read. Grounded theory emphasizes the temporality and process; it calls for a new exploration of every new situation. All interpretations are temporally limited; they are always provisional, immersed in a society and time.

Instead of deriving needs from theory (or from a classification of values and needs), these approaches want to construct a theory of needs based on observed facts such as consumptive choices and consumer interviews. However, in consumer research it might be more relevant to study the subjective meaning of a person's behavior instead of trying to classify him or her on a need scale. We should perhaps study the complex patterns ("motifs") of connotations between a person's inner world and all the objects and other persons in the surrounding outer world.

Through non-systematic learning and reacting, a child develops a complex range of meanings designed by its own biological structure, the behavior of others, and the meanings others ascribe to its behavior. In a child, the cry for food can evolve from a physiological need into a cry for warmth, safety, and security or into a demonstration of emotional solitude or distress (anorexia). Thus, the same motive (say the mother motive of belonging) can be filled in with different meanings and different products.

Behavioral functionalism argues that there might be an indefinite variety of motives underlying an indefinite variety of behavior. In research, this calls for a sensitive methodology capable of discovering the specific pattern of motives that are relevant in a specific consumption context.

Indiana Jones and the Temple of Marketing

The new criteria of postmodern qualitative market research are not very "scientific" at first sight. The academic world does resist it. It would be too personal and far too partisan. Partisan of whom? It would be a veiled form of Marxism or Humanism.

This last reproof is particularly interesting and revealing. Did not Marx himself pretend that his social-economic doctrine was based on dialectic materialism—and that therefore it was scientific? And Humanism? Humanism may not be "scientific," but why does science feel threatened by Humanism? Should science be "politically correct?" To what extent must market research be—and may it be— politically correct?

Postmodern qualitative market research does not want to be politically correct; it should be correct in the eyes of the researcher and in the eyes of the client. Postmodern qualitative market research must be verisimilitudinous and sound truthful. For the authors of the report as well as for the client, the report can and must unlock emotions; for the authors, the emotion of having penetrated to the truth and recognizing themselves; for the client, the emotion of the "A-ha!" experience. The authors must back their report as people with emotions; the client must be able to recognize it as a human, emotional experience.

Postmodern qualitative market research must be ideographic, full, and rich, based on specific cases, detailed interviews, and observation. It is more than research, it is a quest.

No wonder academics reject it as Indiana Jones stories or as journalism.

Postmodern qualitative market research is indeed strongly based on the word, on the story. It is not based on counting noses and not even on questionnaires . . .

• (5): An instrument for interpreting consumer text

The interpretive approach stresses interpretation through the understanding of what some event or text means to the creative actors engaging in it or consuming it. Interpretive understanding of the "subjective experiences" of the consumer needs organizational codes based not on consumer field text alone, but also on the "subjective significance" of the text in terms of need functionality. Illogic does both.

The position of behavioral functionalism on need theory relates closely to a postmodern interpretative approach in qualitative consumer research. In this new era, qualitative researchers are committed to an ideographic, case-based position that directs their attention to the specifics of a particular case. The difference in perspective between casual explanation and interpretative understanding also reflects the concern of Illogic. The interpretative approach stresses interpretation through the understanding of what some event or text means to the creative actors engaged in producing or consuming it.

In this sense, behavioral functionalism argues that "subjective experiences"—the psychological consequences of consumptive behavior—are highly emotional, sometimes unconscious, illogical, fluid, and short-lived.

Understanding the experimental functionality of behavior is highly intuitive and interpretative. It needs organizational codes based not on consumer field text (interview data, observation, materials), but on the "subjective significance" of the text in terms of need functionality.

The objective of the Illogic software is to combine the merits of the two approaches described above: interpretative analysis and structural need theory.

The instrument will use a structural model of consumer motivation in such a way that it helps the analyst form hypotheses concerning a specific complex of consumptive behavior without losing the power of intuitive interpretation and the richness and thickness of consumer text.

In our view, analysis of consumer text, however interpretative and grounded, always at least implicitly has a theory base. The analyst has to decide what constitutes a category, which segments of the text are relevant to that category. The analyst has to decide on the relationship between categories or text segments.

• (6): The basic motivational frame of reference

Two structural dimensions underlie the strategy of Illogic: an individual dimension and a social dimension. The individual dimension represents the classical psychoanalytical concept of tension and repression. The social dimension recognizes the group as a fundamental source of tension and gratification.

Based on cross-cultural experiences in qualitative marketing research, Censydiam developed a model of consumer motivation identifying eight fundamental strategies for need gratification in a consumption context.

We can identify two structural dimensions underlying these strategies: an individual dimension and a social dimension.

The first—individual—dimension represents the classic psychoanalytical concept of release of tension and repression. In conditions of trust, the individual is capable of recognizing specific needs and desires; most of them would be a sublimation of needs or normative adaptations. The individual engages in behavior to satisfy these types of needs as fully and explicitly as he or she can. The individual will liberate the need. However, in conditions of doubt and lack of confidence, the individual will try to control and rationalize particular needs and emotions he or she feels to be threatening or undesirable. The individual will reduce the tension by repressing these needs and desires.

The second—social—dimension recognizes the group as a fundamental source of tension and gratification. On one hand, we can identify the Adlerian concept of struggle for superiority: looking for behavioral solutions that assure superiority over others, external approval and admiration. At the other extreme of this dimension, people want to submit to the needs and expectations of the group, replacing individual desires with the gratification of belonging to a group.

Depending on his or her past life history, a consumer can develop a variety of these strategies with respect to specific products, enabling him or her to manage tension. This portrayal of Man or the basic motivational frame of reference that thus arises can be represented in two-dimensional space.

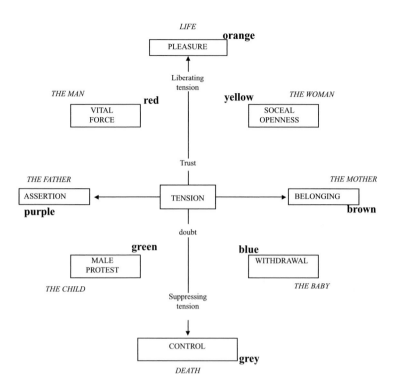

• (7): The interpretive process; the color codes

The researcher is invited to think and feel in terms of motivational hypotheses and understand the subjective experience of the respondent, then assigns a color code to it.

The objective of Illogic is to interpret each significant segment of consumer text as the explication of one of the satisfaction mechanisms that we have mapped in Figure 1, to look for subjective functionality of specific behavior as motives for consumption.

Basically, the instrument asks the analyst to interpret each piece of text as a reference to an underlying strategy of satisfaction, using the eight categories that are visualized as colors. The analyst is invited to think (feel) about the text, to give it need relevance. The analyst is invited to think and feel in terms of motivational hypotheses; to identify the fundamental functionality of the products and brands under research; to understand the subjective experience of the respondent, the psychological release, sublimation, suppression, and displacement it provides.

The figure below lists a number of personality characteristics as they have been interpreted—in a Belgian consumer context—as having meanings corresponding to each of the positions in the frame of reference.

Table 2: Codification of personality traits

Color code	Strategy	Trait	Color code	Strategy	Trait
Orange	Pleasure	Pleasurable Abundant Enjoyable Cheerful	Grey	Control	Defensive Distant Conservative Cold
Yellow	Social openness	Warm Friendly Optimistic Spontaneous	Green	Male protest	Aggressive Extravagant Different Dominant
Brown	Belonging	Trustful Agreeable Nice Modest	Purple	Assertion	Powerful Proud Rich Capable
Blue	Withdrawal	Calm Safe Silent Loyal	Red	Vitality	Vital Active Passionate Energetic

Postmodern qualitative research, "romantic" in the authentic sense of the word

Looking at, interpreting, deciphering . . . the whole interpretative process that we call "field text"—that is what it is all about.

We used to gather information; now there is the exchange between the information that is gathered and the interpretative process. The center has shifted from the data to the interpretative process.

This is no longer about mere data, but about the questions of meaning and social significance. It is no longer a mere enumeration of data, but patterns we find in them, tensions between the different data, and not in the least the narrative threads that run through it. It is no longer a series of steps—circumspect little steps—but a continuous iteration of different data, insights, hypotheses, and so on. Herein the personality of the researcher/analyst plays an important— shall we say decisive—role.

Traditional qualitative research knowingly silences the researcher who had to yield before bare facts. Now the "signature" of the researcher has become almost as important as that of a novelist.

In fact, postmodern qualitative research is "romantic" in the best, the most noble and authentic sense of the word. A novelist worthy of the name bears a heavy responsibility: he or she carries away his/her public to a mental and social world that answers to a deeper reality behind the facts.

The role of the interpreting analysts must go much further than making "analyses." No longer do they give us an outline, the analysis of the story. On the contrary, their story enriches the facts of the outline and transforms them into a coherent whole with a beginning, a middle, and a credible end.

• (8): The interpretive process; coding

An example of how an actual field text is color-coded according to motivational "meaning."

In this same way, the analyst "colors" each relevant text fragment, each observation, each piece of material generated or collected in the field phase. The software provides codes and keys to facilitate this process of coding and reading, recoding and reading again. The use of colors as codes leaves the text fragments literally readable and helps the analyst to think of codes as categories and not as labels or closed boxes.

At the end of each individual text analysis, the analyst has at their disposal a variety of very specific factual texts and their color-coded motivational "meaning."

In the example of Table 1, consumers have been interviewed in a non-directive way on the subject of health and health care.

Table 1: Category codification of consumer interviews on "meaning of health"

Respondent	Strategy / color	Text fragment
Suzanne	VITALITY / RED	You can feel good if you want to.
		Health means exercising the body. It needs to move. We sit still too much.
		We are like animals. We have to move, otherwise the muscles weaken and the heart cannot continue to beat.
		Moving. Riding a bicycle.
		Energy creates more energy. Cycling. Running.
		You become alert and energetic.
		The ideal would be to live in the countryside, to work with your body, to breathe clean air; to me it means to move, to feel good on all levels.
	SOCIAL OPEN-NESS / YELLOW	Health by having a good social life, not only watching TV.
		Walking, going to a bar or something.
		Important to have exterior stimuli, to do things that make you feel good, like when you feel like going out.
		Just feel good.

	WITHDRAWL / BLUE I	I used to control my health by eating vegetarian food.
		Not McDonald's, no Coke; I try to avoid these things; I drink water.
Ann	ASSERTION / PURPLE I	I used to participate in swimming competitions. I did a lot of exercise.
		I wanted to look thin and therefore I smoked. Now I managed to quit smoking.
		I need to be healthy because I have a demanding executive job.
	MALE PROTEST / GREEN	I do not eat correctly and I lead a stressful life. I come home, have to go out again, and do not feel like cooking for myself; I just eat a TV dinner.
		I have to jog and work out in a gymnasium as a counterpart of my busy professional life.
		I need to eat products that have enough yin and yang: fresh, raw, primary products.
		Being healthy also means looking good, having a nice body and a nice tan.
	BELONGING / BROWN	My mom tried to think of the way the Weight Watchers cook and eat, I tried it, and it works.
		To eat right is not eating sweets or potato chips.
		Eating cooked food without fat as often as possible, no cream and that sort of thing.
		My mom always says that eating domestic food keeps you healthy.
Peder	WITHDRAWAL / BLUE	Calm atmosphere: not to become a teacher.
		Living in a calm place, in the country, not in a big city.
		Not working on a computer all day long.
		Not having to worry about things all the time has an effect on the whole mechanism of the body.
	CONTROL / GREY	If I am hungry, I eat chocolate, and then my friends tell me to eat a banana instead.
		It often happens that I do not eat the right food, but that is easier said than done.
		My health is not good enough; it sometimes frightens me.

The postmodern researcher/analyst, the Victor Hugo of market research

The first exposition at the new national library in Paris, *Très Grande Bibliothèque,* showed manuscripts of great writers. One could literally see and follow how important novels of the 19th and 20th centuries came into being. One could see the notes, the material of the *nouveaux romans.*

We can best compare our reports with the *nouveau roman*—the postmodern novel.

Whereas the manuscripts of the classical novel—take those of Balzac or Hugo—are overcrowded with corrections, retrocession, parts that are completely overwritten, the postmodern novelist works without deletions straight through to the end. Indeed, they always have at their disposal a "display text" in order to arrive at an "analytic text," they have a complete set of data to which they can keep referring.

Victor Hugo may be the first author who used "field data," namely puppets of his characters that he placed on his worktable because otherwise—with the multitude of characters he had to control—he could not remember how they fit together in his story.

The postmodern researcher/analyst works in the same way.

There is a continuous dialogue between ideas and facts on which he or she relies in order to come—after necessary corrections along the way—to a valuable and credible theory.

In his or her specific report, the researcher/analyst will work from an abstract to a plausible theory. He or she will identify themes, patterns, and clusters. He or she will suggest comparisons. He or she will integrate the connections he or she accordingly finds within one whole. He or she will suggest interpretations, interpretations that in their turn can be tested against other cases, with other material.

- (9): Displaying the "illogics"

Identifying consistencies and certainly inconsistencies ("illogics") will invite the analyst to form hypotheses, review coding, and begin to understand the need functionality of the respondent's behavior. Some examples . . .

After encoding is finished, a kaleidoscope of colors is attached to each respondent's text. Comparing color codes within the text of each respondent and across respondents on specific behavioral cues, products, and brands to identify consistencies and certainly inconsistencies ("illogics") will invite the analyst to form hypotheses, review coding, and begin to understand the need functionality of the behavior.

One of the tools in this analysis is a little statistic that counts the number of colors used within a respondent's text and presents it in the form of a pie chart. This helps the analyst discover the leading strategy of the respondent, as well as discover "illogic" color combinations.

In our example, there seems to be an "illogic" between the red/orange text of Suzanne and her blue coded text on health. Anne has a very "illogic" profile of purple/green, indicating the need to manage health in a very dominant and analytic way versus brown where she wants to submit to the caring and normative demands of her environment (her mother). Peder shows little illogic: blue and gray dominate his profile.

Now the analyst is forced to go back to the segments of text and understand these "illogics," thereby creating insight into the specific satisfaction mechanism at work. Once the "implicit" meaning of text fragments has been established, more traditional codification techniques can be applied to specify the need-functional mechanisms at play.

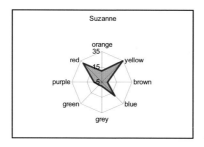

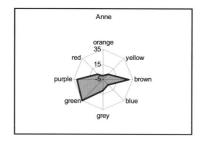

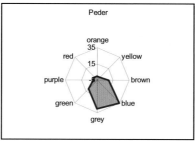

For Dr. Spock maybe, but not for Censydiam

The concept of behavioral functionalism, says Professor Helmut Gaus, implies that all consumptive behavior must be seen in a definite context and understood as being functional with respect to underlying needs.

Our analyses must not concentrate on behavior itself, but on the effect it has on the need-state of the consumer. This requires a precise and detailed description of the subjective "meaning" and an understanding of the individual experience of the effects or consequences of this behavior.

Those "functional experiences" are highly emotional, and sometimes unconscious, illogical, floating, and short-lived, but are always—up to a point—also cognitive. Therefore, understanding these "functional experiences" is highly intuitive and interpretive.

For this, we need organizational codes that are based not on data we have gathered by means of interviews and observation, but on the "subjective significance" of these data in terms of need-functionality, subjective "meaning" having nothing to do with statistical significance.

One of the tools we use to that end at Censydiam is our Illogic software.

• (10): Typology of the need functionality of consumer behavior

Conclusions as to the example of health: people experience health as something one-dimensional and focus on the illness that needs to be cured; a second dimension reflects on how people deal with the significance of health as a sign toward their environment.

In the case of health care (using verbatim consumer text on self-image and meaning of health), we found that in conditions of trust people tend to develop a holistic, constructive approach to health where maximization of life becomes the goal. However, when doubt dominates, people need to control and repress their existential anxiety in order to survive emotionally. Health is experienced as something one-dimensional. These people focus more on the illness that needs to be cured.

A second dimension reflects how people deal with the significance of health (of being healthy or sick) as a sign toward their relevant environment. We see how some people approach health in a very analytical, active, and individual way. Health is a means to show self-confidence, to stand out from the crowd. For others, being healthy is a means to fit in with the environment, to live up to the social norm around health. Health is getting meaning on a collective level, it is a means to be part of the group. Here one deals more passively, more intuitively with health.

On the analytical frame of reference map, this need functionality situates itself as such:

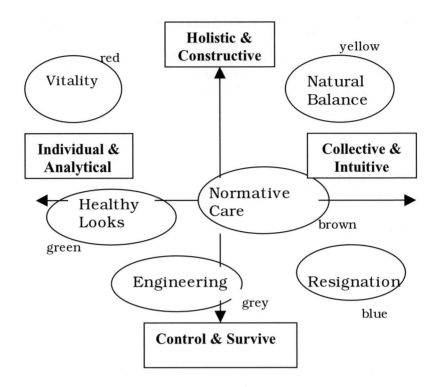

• (11): Advantages, limitations, and future development

Illogic protects the analyst from relying too heavily on first impressions and hasty conclusions. By offering solid documentation, easily accessible text fragments, and analytical transparency, Illogic improves acceptance of cross-cultural comparative analysis of consumer data.

The advantage of this instrument is that it gives easy access to a conceptual level of analysis by creating a second level of interpretive text. Textual structure is related to theoretical "content" by means of conceptual operators, visualized in colors. It generates "meaning" while respecting the richness of the text itself. It allows the writer to build insight and understanding while staying very close to the actual text. Moreover, the structural base and the coding procedures reduce some of the practical objections to some interpretive work applied to consumer data, i.e. the high level of writer influence. Users of consumer analysis often need a very high degree of positivist reassurance in the form of low-level statistics and inter-analyst consistency. The Illogic procedure also protects the analyst from relying too heavily on first impressions and early conclusions. It reduces the prominence of dramatic incidents and flamboyant text fragments. By offering solid documentation, easily accessible text fragments, and analytical transparency, the method improves acceptance of cross-cultural comparative analysis of consumer data.

However, the instrument does not pretend to solve the problem of "representation" in qualitative research. Qualitative research can never "directly" capture the human experience in social text. Yet, we do think that the note-taking module, the color coding, and the analytical module provide a very close connection between the written report and the life experience of respondents. The objective remains small-scale analysis of specific behavior in a specific context.

In future developments, we will try to answer the realistic user's demand for stability and comparability interpretive analysis. In this respect, training of analysts, case studies, and possibly parallel coding by two or more analysts are important. We could also propose the development of a culture-specific thesaurus of color coding, based on the growing number of applied analyses in different consumer areas and cultures. The drawback is that it might limit the intuitive creativity of the analyst when he or she is confronted with a computer suggesting a color to interpret a text fragment.

Diane Op de Beeck

9. Future watch

Or why yesterday tells us
of tomorrow

Professor Helmut Gaus has discovered long-term cyclical patterns of consumer "insecurity" that can be used to help forecast economic trends. His theory is rooted in the fact that a major part of our behavior is determined not by reason, but by subconscious processes. If we are forced to explain our behavior, we will hardly ever admit such a thing. Instead, we will try to find a rationalization. These unconscious processes, however, drive consumer behavior and can be used in aggregate to understand the antecedents of good and bad economic times.

• (1): "I hope that this theory is false. I fear that it is correct."

Prof. Helmut Gaus' theory is rooted in the fact that a major part of our behavior is not determined by reason but by subconscious processes. If we are forced to explain our behavior, we will hardly ever admit that; we will try to find a rationalization.

That is what Prof. Dr. Helmut Gaus put as a motto at the beginning of his book on the significance of long waves to our knowledge of people's behavior in society.

As soon as we are confronted with a theory, Prof. Gaus says, we react to it on the basis of the individual background, knowledge, opinions, and preconceptions we already have in our heads. All this will determine our overall judgment of the theory. When people from different disciplines—i.e. with very different academic backgrounds—are confronted with the same theory, their understanding and judgment will largely be determined by these backgrounds.

Our theory is rooted in the fact that a major part of our behavior is determined not by reason, but by subconscious processes. Carl Gustav Jung expressed it concisely when he said that consciousness was an island in the sea of the subconscious. In other words, before anything comes to the surface of our consciousness, it was already there.

Many motives behind our behavior are not the result of conscious thinking. For a psychologist this is, of course, as evident as can be. There are quite a few people, however, who will raise their eyebrows when they hear this. Is reason no longer the only true instrument of explanation?

If we are forced to explain our behavior to another person, we will hardly ever admit that we do not really know why we behave in a particular way. We will try to find a rationalization and, in addition, we will—unwittingly—seek an extra rationalization that we—subconsciously—suppose the other person will understand and accept. Whether these rationalizations are true or not is another question. That is why we pay particular attention in this study to what people do and only sporadically to what they think and what they say.

• (2): Is people's behavior non-recurrent?

We are not dealing with the behavior of individuals but of the masses, or large sections of society. If we assume that human behavior is a reaction to external circumstances, we must also assume that changes of circumstances will result in changes of behavior. In this reasoning, behavior is non-recurrent.

Behavioral information is our keyword. However, this creates the problem of how to interpret this behavior, of establishing what it means. Furthermore: what is the accuracy of our interpretation? Which theories shall we use? All of this does not make it any easier.

In addition, we are dealing not with the subconscious behavior of individuals, but of the masses, or more correctly, of large sections of society. If in a span of a few years, groups appear in the political landscape that begin to worry about the environment, they display a behavior that makes their views clear: periodicals will appear, associations will be formed, Green Parties will get thousands of votes, and so on. We call this mass behavior because it concerns large parts of the masses. This is a convention. Accordingly, when we talk of behavior of large sections of those masses, we talk in fact of averages.

The second remark relates to the distinction between human behavior and the circumstances in which people live. This distinction is to some extent arbitrary, but then again, it is vital to our theory.

This is what we are talking about: on one hand, there is the evolution of the circumstances in which people lived and live. The circumstances change over the years according to their own time and rhythm, such as population growth during the last 2,000 years, discoveries, inventions, and so on. The external context in which people lived 2,000 years ago is barely similar to the circumstances in which they live now.

If we assume that human behavior is reactive, i.e. a reaction to the external circumstances in which people live, we must also assume that the constant changes of circumstances will result in a constant change of behavior, and that the behavior of contemporary people is in no way comparable with behavior in the past.

In this reasoning, all behavior is non-recurring and so it does not allow scientific study in the strict sense of the word science, according to which uniqueness is a contradiction in terms.

• (3): Brutus murdered Caesar only once, but . . .

This preconception of non-recurrent behavior prevents us from learning anything from human behavior in the past. Our central theme is anxiety-driven behavior in the present and in the past. Recurrent behavior may have few supporters in the science of history; in historical economics, it is the very basis.

If behavior is non-recurring, we could indeed argue that Brutus murdered Julius Caesar on one occasion only. Yet, if we want to make a scientific study of regicide, we can start with Caesar and end, for example, with John F. Kennedy. So we can compare hundreds of regicides from the past.

The suggestion that there are constants in human behavior that can be traced back to Roman or even prehistoric times conflicts with two tenacious preconceptions of our era: the preconception of linear progress, which since the end of the 18th century has replaced the idea of a more cyclical evolution, and the preconception that we have become the "smartest" in history today (simply because we are still alive and the others are dead). These two preconceptions prevent us from learning anything from human behavior in the past and call behavioral historical science a utopia.

For the most part, however, these preconceptions are implicitly rather than explicitly present; they are hardly ever conscious. The past is an immensely rich laboratory of human behavior. The contemporary, living human being cannot imagine behavior that would not have hundreds of parallels in history.

Our central theme is anxiety-driven behavior in the present and in the past, and it could well happen that more than a few people will be prepared to accept—in spite of all preconceptions—that it is almost certainly a subject for all eras.

A third remark concerns repeats, or recurrences, or models, or systems of human behavior, or whatever one wants to call them. On one hand, it is a subject everyone is familiar with in daily life, but on the other hand, it is also a delicate subject, depending on the discipline in natural sciences. In the science of history, it has no more than a few supporters, whereas it is widely accepted in psychology and sociology. In historical economics, it is the very basis.

• (4): Will the West decline? Will civilizations clash?

The remarkable thing about psychology is that recurrences are accepted in the case of individual deviant behavior, , but one is much more reserved when large groups or masses are concerned.

People's behavior consists of many repetitions, recurrent behavioral patterns, which can even be represented by models. Social scientists generally content themselves with finding these recurrences—which is no easy task in itself, considering the continually changing parameters. Yet, recurrences in human behavior are so much more important in view of the study of prognoses and, in history, retrognoses, too—by which we mean "prognoses in the past." For example, if we find certain behavior in a certain context, similar behavior must have occurred in similar contexts in a distant past.

In everyday life, we incessantly observe our fellow humans. Slowly but surely, we see certain patterns of behavior recur: certain ways of thinking, of acting, of reacting. Taken together, we often call these "someone's character," and that, after all, is a construction. With this knowledge, we can make the prognosis that if such a person with these personality traits finds himself in a certain situation, he will very probably behave in the way we already know.

As a science, psychology is based on this principle. Deviant behavior is observed and then we study how someone who shows such deviant behavior behaves. After studying a number of cases, we assume that someone with such an abnormality will display this behavior—which is a prognosis.

The remarkable thing about this is that, at the level of the individual or of small groups, one is ready to accept and also use these recurrences, whereas one is much more reserved when large groups or masses are concerned.

Whether the West will decline, as Oswald Spengler says, or civilizations will clash, as Francis Fukuyama predicts, are questions that also imply prognoses about the evolution of external circumstances. Well, we do not have the faintest idea of how to make a prognosis about the discovery of nuclear fusion with tap water as a new source of energy, for example, though it would have immense consequences for the evolution of the whole world.

- (5): Nicolai Kondratiev's discovery of the long waves pleases the Marxists

In the early twenties, the Russian economist Kondratiev found a cyclic pattern of approximately 50 years in the evolution of wholesale prices: prices lowered for 25 years and rose again for the next 25 years. Economists tried to give an explanation for the fact, which appeared to be entirely economical. They were wrong.

Since the beginning of the 20th century, the only ones who have always kept a watchful eye on the behavior of groups over a longer period with a view to find recurrences have been economists, with Nicolai Kondratiev in front.

In the early twenties, the Russian economist Kondratiev discovered that there was a definite pattern in the evolution of wholesale prices. He calculated those prices from the end of the 18th century until his own times and found that they showed a cyclic pattern of approximately 50 years, i.e. one cycle every half century. It emerged that prices rose for 25 years and fell again for the next 25 years.

The discovery that prices went up and down in a regular cycle was completely new, and this held significant promise, as it would enable us to forecast future upward and downward phases.

It is clear that these observations raised several questions in economists' minds. What caused this cyclic development? More importantly, from an economic point of view, how dependable were the forecasts now made possible? The fact that purely economic explanations were sought with regard to a phenomenon, which, admittedly, appeared to be entirely economic, is the very reason why the research has not yielded universally accepted answers. The economists are still pursuing their quest.

However, we should also note that the general state of the world differed greatly between ascending and descending phases. Especially in the downward phases, it was clear that cultural, political, social, and warlike behavior showed great similarity.

In Kondratiev's time, and especially for the Marxists, it was logical to ascribe this similarity to the state of the market: as the upward and downward economic trends establish themselves, people can be expected to adjust their behavior accordingly. In short, the whole phenomenon served to prove once more, in Marxist phraseology, the omnipotence of the infrastructure over the superstructure.

However, as we have seen, Marxists have not always been right . . .

- (6): Which comes first, economy or anxiety?

In fact, what Kondratiev had discovered was the effect of fluctuations in societal anxiety on wholesale prices. Though not strong enough to reach a conscious level, this angst is present at all levels of society and influences values, norms, behavior, mentality, et cetera, during the ascending and descending periods of anxiety.

If it was the declining economy that inspired more cautious behavior, how could it be that people began to act more cautiously even before the decline of the economy set in? Conversely, how was it that people became more optimistic before the economic data justified such behavior?

Decades of longitudinal data gathering on the most diverse forms of human behavior gradually yielded one conclusion that could explain the great variety of behavior in different—mostly not economic—fields. What Kondratiev had discovered was the effect of fluctuations in societal anxiety on wholesale prices.

Alternatively, the real discovery here is the existence of an average level of insecurity or existential fear in society. Though not strong enough to reach a conscious level, this angst is nevertheless present at all levels of society and has a profound influence on values, norms, behavior, mentality, interests, etc., during an ascending or descending period.

The peaks in the economic climate (such as in the late sixties and early seventies) are periods with a very low level of insecurity. High average levels of angst, on the other hand, can be seen when the economy is at its lowest, such as the late eighties and early nineties. This also makes it clear why the causes of the long waves, or more precisely the causes of the switch at a peak or a trough, are not economic and must therefore be sought outside the economic frame of reference.

At the peak of an economic boom, when economic euphoria reigns, people suddenly start to feel insecure: the pendulum of angst has swung; they moderate their consumption. Hence they cause a recession that, once started, develops its own dynamic. The latter, in turn, is further strengthened by the simultaneously and constantly growing uncertainty and angst in society. Once the vicious circle is complete, it becomes impossible to establish whether it is the psychological or economic facts that continue to push the economy upward or downward. Whatever economic measures one applies, the evolution of existential fear cannot be reversed; it can at most be mitigated for a limited period.

- (7): Interpreting behavior of large groups both in the past and in the future

Taking this new point of departure, the more explicit knowledge of anxiety and anxious behavior dictates the domains of behavior of groups and masses that qualify for research. Types of behavior that at first sight are unrelated become evident when explained because of anxiety.

Applying the cycles of existential fear, of angst, enables considerable progress to be made in the interpretation of the behavior of large groups and masses both in the past and now.

After all, many types of behavior cannot be linked directly to economic recessions, but they can be recognized as a form of anxiety behavior that expresses itself, for example, through demands for stricter norms, increasing egocentrism, or a multitude of identity crises.

Taking this new point of departure, the more explicit knowledge of anxiety and anxious behavior more or less dictates the domains and areas of the behavior of groups and masses that qualify for research. This is an enormous gain in the heuristic field for a number of types of behavior that at first sight are unrelated, but become evident since they can be explained by anxiety.

Yet it is not for the explanation of people's behavior in the past and the present that the knowledge of the cyclic evolution of basic anxiety is the most valuable; its crucial value lies in the now possible knowledge of the behavior of large groups and masses in the future.

If it was meaningful for economists to know that prices have followed a definite pattern and will follow it tomorrow, it is crucially significant for any student of the behavior of groups and masses to know that, as in the past, this behavior in the future will be determined by "cycles" of existential fear.

This trend may be interrupted for a short time by particular events, and even by some years of worldwide economic recession. Yet, if the peaks of the waves of anxiety continue to behave as they did in the past, we must expect another twenty or fifteen-year decrease in the average level of societal anxiety. According to this cyclic pattern of explanation, the next economic peak—the phase with the least existential fear and uncertainty—can be anticipated around the year 2020.

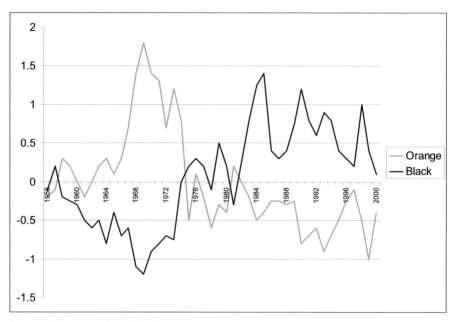

Source: Why Yesterday tells of tomorrow

The long waves of anxiety (black) and the long waves of optimism and self-assurance (orange) ascertained by means of the dominance of orange/yellow colors and black colors dominating in fashion over the years. They correspond with other fashion characteristics such as long versus short skirts, high versus low necklines, depending on whether we find ourselves at the top or are the bottom of the long wave of anxiety.

• (8): We will soon dominate domination and withdrawal

Some examples of what lies in store for us in the immediate future, or why and how yesterday tells us of tomorrow . . .

What sort of behavior may we expect when angst increases and what behavior will subside when anxiety wanes?

Relations with fellow human beings are, of course, to a greater degree determined by the amount of anxiety or uncertainty in society. People need other people to assert themselves, to know how they should value themselves. The fear of anxious people consists precisely of the fear that they will not get this confirmation. The painful result is that they find it more secure to withdraw from others so others cannot make them feel worthless.

Basic anxiety thus contains the seed of a potential conflict between longing for others, longing to rely on them, and the inability to do so. This brings us to the paradoxical situation that during the phases in which one needs others most, the communication with those others is more difficult to establish and more superficial than during phases in which one has less need for others, i.e. when there is less anxiety in society. People are willing to bear a lot to ensure the affection of others, including submission to other people's wishes.

This is important because of the common assumption that submission is always imposed by the authorities. It is the other way round. Submitting to the authorities can create a "good feeling." Thus, obeying the rules, living in accordance with the norms, can become a determined pursuit corresponding to an underlying motivation.

During the long upward curve of the economy, which now lies ahead, this need for authority and power will gradually diminish as the level of anxiety falls. The areas in which liberty is pursued will greatly extend. Options that are not imaginable today will be claimed tomorrow. The individual will begin to experience a new self-esteem.

There will, of course, always be over-anxious and under-anxious people, but the size of such groups will greatly change as the level of societal anxiety lowers. How soon this will happen and in which domains of behavior it will happen first are questions that longitudinal research cannot answer.

10. Four case studies

Or how to sell bad news

Following are several case studies that illustrate the importance of the unconscious to consumer choice and hence motivational market research.

• (1): Multiple roles of affect in persuading the consumer, or how to sell bad news

Emotions play an important role in marketing products or services. Here we focus on the role of affective valence (i.e. the attraction or aversion that an individual feels toward a specific object or event) on the consumers' persuasion process. Can the use of negative feelings still have a beneficial effect in an advertising campaign?

In order to show you how different Censydiam case studies can be from "classical" case studies, we want to quote from Dr. Anick Bosmans' doctoral thesis. Bosmans is now a doctor of Applied Economics, which—as you will remember—is another term for marketing.

The title of her thesis, which she defended at the Research Center for Consumer Psychology and Marketing at the University of Ghent (Belgium) in which Censydiam was also involved, is *Affective Persuasive Communication: Multiple Roles of Affect in Persuading the Consumer.*

Emotions play an important role in the marketing of products and services, she writes. Despite the extensive practical applications, the explanatory mechanisms are often not very clear and straightforward. Researchers have found that positive feelings—e.g. elicited by a pleasant odor or by a pleasant movie—lead to more positive product evaluations.

The opposite seems to hold for negative feelings, she suggests. However, these findings cannot account for the beneficial effects that are usually observed when advertisers and marketers use negative feelings such as guilt and sadness in their advertising campaigns.

Dr. Bosmans argues that there are multiple roles for affect. She focused on the role of affective valence (i.e. the attraction or aversion that an individual feels toward a specific object or event) on the consumers' persuasion process.

According to socio-psychological literature, she says, most people seem to act to maintain their positive moods while avoiding being in a negative mood.

- **(2): Positive mood, negative mood . . . what effect do affects have?**

People in a negative mood are more likely to engage in systematic processing of the information presented, i.e. the advertisement. People also use their current feelings as the basis for forming evaluations, i.e. they take their current feelings as informative material.

Since processing a message extensively often results in feelings of aversion for the task (especially when the task is difficult), says Dr. Bosmans, message recipients in a positive mood are motivated to avoid such thorough processing in order to maintain their positive moods.

In contrast, a negative mood signals that the situation is problematic. Something has to be done in order to change the situation. Therefore, people in a negative mood are more likely to engage in systematic processing of the information presented.

Another way in which affect can influence the consumers' persuasion process is by coloring consumers' thoughts while they are evaluating a new brand or a new product. This is most likely when consumers are very motivated to process the advertisement, the commercial, or the sales talk. Happy people will therefore recall more material that is pleasant and make more positive evaluations. But is the reverse also true?

It is true that when people were not very motivated to process the ad, the study found evidence for "affect as information." This "affect as information" hypothesis suggests that people sometimes use their current feelings as the basis for forming evaluations. That is, when people make an evaluation, they sometimes mistakenly take their current feelings as informative material. They seem to think: "I feel good, so the product/brand must be good."

Dr. Bosmans used a variety of affective stimuli—including both affect elicited by the ad and the consumer's general mood state—throughout her dissertation, which consistently showed evidence for the multiple roles of affect on consumers' evaluation processes.

But how did she do that? How do you "measure" such a thing as affective persuasion?

- (3): Will unhappiness also breed contempt? Or otherwise?

Advertisers and marketers often have to deal with products or services that are associated with negative beliefs or feelings. The main purpose of these case studies is to explore consumers' evaluations of such products and services.

The studies we present here investigate the effect of affective valence on consumers' evaluations of product categories that are associated with negative beliefs and feelings. In the first two studies, the participants' moods were manipulated. They were confronted with an ad for a service (blood donation) and a product category (condoms) that have negative connotations.

Advertisers and marketers often have to deal with products and services that are associated with negatively valenced beliefs or feelings. The main purpose of the following studies is to explore consumers' evaluations of such products and services. An essentially emotionally neutral ad for a painkiller, for example, is very likely to call for negative valence: thoughts of painful headaches, stomach complaints, and the like. The mere thought of using a sedative is associated with these negative representations. In a related vein, a governmental campaign for blood donation will probably evoke mental images of dizziness, a sore arm, nausea, and so on.

More specifically, the studies aim to investigate the influence of the affective status (e.g. being in a happy or sad mood; being positively or negatively affected by the advertisements) on the evaluation of these negative product/service categories.   For example, campaigns concerning charity—such as organizations against child abuse or organizations helping developing countries—often try to elicit feelings of sadness or guilt. These negative valences are often consistent with people's mental representation (one's mental scheme) of child abuse or developing countries.

Will a "sad charity commercial" lead to better evaluative effect than a "happy charity commercial" in this context? Will evaluation be more positive when one is in a negative mood when evaluating a new brand of painkiller, or will they, on the contrary, be more positive when they are in a positive mood?

- (4): Gaining more insight into the persuasion process

A number of theoretical frameworks can be invoked to come up with theoretically based expectations regarding the influence of affective states on the evaluation of negative products or services. In the next pages, we will discuss three important frameworks: affect priming, affect as information, and cognitive tuning.

The first two studies investigate the influence of mood as a more global and nonspecific affective state on the evaluation of negative valence material categories. The last two studies will focus on the effects of consumers' affects—resulting from an emotionally laden advertisement—on the evaluation of the product concerned.

We believe that insight into the underlying mechanisms of the evaluation of negative valence is of more than practical importance. Past studies of mood effect on persuasion measured exclusively evaluations of products or services associated with neutral or positive valence. In the following studies, it is argued that more insight into the persuasion process can be gained when considering products that are likely to call for negatively valenced association.

A number of theoretical frameworks can be invoked in order to come up with theoretically based expectations regarding the influence of affective states on the evaluation of negative products or services. In the next sections, we will discuss what appear to us to be the three most common theoretical frameworks in the field of affective persuasion: affect priming, affect as information, and cognitive tuning.

All of these models originate from social psychology. Only recently were some attempts made to translate these models into a context of consumer behavior and marketing. In what follows, it becomes clear that those different theoretical considerations predict different outcomes when it comes to mood effects on the evaluation of products/services with negative valence. In the case of evaluating positive or neutral products or services, however, note that all those frameworks predict the same outcome, namely mood-congruent judgments. Nevertheless, is that always true?

• (5): Affect priming leads to mood-corresponding evaluations

Affect priming. A positive or a negative mood cues similar valence in memory. A positive mood provides more positive product evaluations because of the accessibility of positive material and reduces overall capacity available for other tasks, such as evaluation of the message of the advertisement.

According to the affect-priming hypothesis, positive or negative mood states cue similarly valenced material in memory, thereby biasing people's perception of the target at the time of the evaluation. Hence, when in a positive mood, activation will spread towards related positive valences, resulting in a more positive evaluation compared to when the mood is more negative or neutral.

The ultimate consequence of the induction of a positive mood is that it (1) provides more positive product evaluations as a result of the accessibility of positive material and (2) reduces the overall capacity available for other tasks or leads to a more heuristic form of processing of the primary evaluation task due to reduced processing capacity.

Affect priming is most likely observed when people are relatively highly motivated to process the information, i.e. as the case may be for the message of the advertisement. Especially when the processing motivation is high, the mood-colored thoughts will be taken into account when making an evaluation. In other words, a positive mood increases the ultimate positiveness of the thoughts generated.

Because highly motivated people are more likely to consider their thoughts when making an evaluation, we can expect that our results are consistent with the affect-priming hypothesis, especially when the likelihood to process the information is high.

Applied to our current research, we can therefore expect that evaluations of our negatively valenced product/service will be more positive under positive mood conditions since more positive material is expected to become accessible in memory: according to affect priming, mood-corresponding evaluations are expected.

• (6): Affect as information or "How do I feel about it?"

Affect as information. Although the underlying mechanism is different from the affect-priming hypothesis, the affect-as-information model also predicts that evaluations will be more positive when people are in a positive mood. Hence, affect as information also predicts mood-corresponding judgments.

According to the affect-as-information model, people sometimes mistake the affective feedback that is provided by their current mood state for the affective feedback they experience when evaluating a target stimulus. That is, people sometimes mistake aspects of their reactions to a non-target source as their reaction to the target.

One consequence of this is a shift of people's target evaluation toward the valence of their moods—i.e. mood-corresponding judgments. This process, whereby mood is seen as informative for the judgment to be made, has been labeled in literature as the "How do I feel about it?" heuristic.

Mood influences judgments—such as judgments of satisfaction with life—only when affective cues of the mood are perceived as informative, in that they appear to be part of the reaction to the object of judgment. In other words, mood will have such effects only when respondents do not make external attributions for their feelings.

It has been shown that taking one's affect as a source of information is the result of a decreased processing motivation: when respondents are explicitly instructed to pay attention to the strength of the argument (i.e. increasing one's motivation), people base their evaluations on the strength of the arguments and no longer on their own affective state. Hence, when motivation to process increases, the affect-as-information effect disappears.

Although the underlying mechanism is different from the affect-priming hypothesis, the affect-as-information model also predicts that evaluations will be more positive when people are in a positive mood. Hence, affect as information also predicts mood-corresponding judgments.

- (7): Cognitive tuning, or positive evaluations when the mood is negative and vice versa

Cognitive tuning is a "cognitive" extension of the affect-as-information hypothesis; it assumes that affective cues also provide procedural information. Opposite results are expected from affect-priming and affect-as-information processes: more positive evaluations when the mood is negative and vice versa.

The cognitive-tuning hypothesis, which can be seen as a "cognitive" extension of the affect-as-information hypothesis, assumes that affective cues provide not only substantive, but also procedural information. A cognitive-tuning effect occurs when feedback about the nature of a situation modifies how information is processed.

Negative cues—such as negative moods—signal that a problem has been encountered and that the ongoing efforts and strategies are inadequate. Conversely, positive affective cues signal that a situation is benign and that one's current effort and strategies are adequate. More positive affective cues could therefore elicit less systematic and more heuristic processing.

Given the tendency of happy individuals toward parsimonious and effortless processing, it is not so surprising that happy individuals seem to rely on general knowledge structures. Because general knowledge structures allow the individual to reduce the complexity of information processing at different stages, they often promote parsimonious and efficient processing.

If we apply this reasoning to our research problem with regard to the effects of affect on negatively valenced mental schemata, we can expect that subjects in a positive mood will make evaluations that are more negative. This is because they base their evaluations on a knowledge structure that is loaded with negative affect. The contrary is also true, as we will see when we discuss the ads for a new meat label. First, the reactions are negative because of the recent meat crisis, and then they turn positive when one thinks of it more systematically.

Hence, opposite results are expected from cognitive tuning than from affect-priming or affect-as-information processes; namely, more positive evaluations when the mood is negative and more negative evaluations when the mood is positive.

• (8): Blood donation, how the study was made

Before being presented with the ad, the respondents were assigned to two mood conditions by assigning them to write an account of either a happy or a sad life event. After viewing the ad, the respondents' reactions were measured on four different scales.

The purpose of this first study was to explore the proposed effect of mood (positive versus negative) on the evaluation of a category with negative valence. We expected that at least one of the aforementioned frameworks would be able to explain the observed effects.

The participants were 46 undergraduate students. They volunteered for what was presented as an advertising study. None had ever donated blood before.

The participants were randomly assigned to one of the two mood conditions. We explained briefly that they were to complete some independent tasks, which included (a) the mood induction, (b) presentation of the critical ad concerning a blood donation initiative, and (c) measurement of the dependent variable: evaluation of the initiative.

For the mood induction task, the participants were asked to provide a vivid written report of either a happy or a sad life event, purportedly unrelated with the remaining tasks.

After this mood induction, subjects were presented with an advertisement describing a new—i.e. fictitious—blood donation initiative organized by the university. The initiative stated that, as of the following year, every student would be obliged to donate blood at least once a year. After this statement, some arguments promoting the blood donation initiative were given. The respondents were given one minute to look at the ad.

After presentation of the ad, the dependent variable as well as an additional mood manipulation variable were measured. The respondents were asked, "How do you feel at this moment?" and answers had to be given on a nine-point scale ranging from extremely bad to extremely good. This was done to make sure that our mood manipulation lasted as long as the ad was presented. Evaluation of the blood donation initiative was measured on four seven-point semantic differential items: positive/negative, love/hate, good/bad, and desirable/undesirable. Lower scores indicated less positive attitudes.

- (9): Blood donation, how the advertisement was perceived

Blood donation, the results. Affect priming was observed in our positive mood condition and cognitive tuning was observed in our negative mood condition. As long as consumers have sufficient processing motivation, both positive and negative moods would lead to more positive evaluations when the product has negative connotations.

No effects of mood on the evaluation of the blood donation initiative were found. Hence, no support for affective persuasion was obtained.

It is important to note that our blood donation schema was a very negative one. Several subjects reported feeling nauseous and dizzy when looking at the ad and thinking about the blood donation initiative. This negativity alone may have resulted in the fact that people's affective status in all our experimental conditions became so negative that the negativity of the mental schema alone overrode all other mood effects. In other words, we might have been confronted with a floor effect.

Another possibility is that the processing motivation was too high for mood effects to take place, resulting in a ceiling effect.

The lack of solid explanation for our null findings made us think (although post hoc) that maybe mood did affect persuasion, but that the effects were present in both our positive as well as in our negative mood conditions, hence filtering out any observable effects. In this case, two different mechanisms are expected to be responsible for these effects: active in both mood conditions. Hence, evaluations in both positive *and* negative mood conditions may be more positive than in a neutral control condition.

Since we can safely assume that all our respondents were highly motivated, we suggest that *affect priming* was observed in our positive mood condition (since affect priming is mostly found under conditions of high processing motivation) and *cognitive tuning* was observed in our negative mood condition.

From a practical point of view, this reasoning would suggest that, as long as consumers have sufficient processing motivation, both positive as well as negative moods would lead to more positive evaluations when the product has negative connotations.

• (10): Condoms, how the study was made

Condoms are less negative a subject than blood donation. Involvement of the respondents was manipulated to obtain low- and a high-processing motivation conditions. The mood manipulation check was the same as in the previous study.

This study was made to further test the post hoc explanation of Case 1. We used a product category with negative valence that was not as negative as our blood donation initiative, in order to prevent our respondents from being too motivated to process because of the negative effect. We also manipulated involvement to obtain a low- and high-processing motivation condition.

If our post hoc explanation holds, we should again find no effect of mood on persuasion if processing motivation is high, but we should find it if processing motivation is low: we should then find results consistent with the affect-as-information condition. Moreover, since we expect that affect priming as well as cognitive tuning are at play under conditions of high processing motivation, we expect the evaluations in both mood conditions will be more positive compared to baseline levels.

Processing motivation was manipulated using different involving instructions. In the high-involvement condition, we told the participants that *their* university was thinking about setting up a campaign about condom use because prior research had shown that their students did not have safe sex. Besides, we asked respondents to look carefully because their university wanted the campaign to be effective given the high costs involved.

In the low-involvement condition, respondents were told that *another* university was doing some research about how people looked at advertisements.

After these involvement instructions, the critical ad was presented. Depending upon advertisement type condition, the ad was either textual or visual. The brand name Flexus is an imaginary name.

After the presentations of the ads, we measured the dependent variable as well as a mood manipulation check and an involvement check. The mood manipulation check was the same as in the previous study.

- (11): Condoms, how they were perceived

Condoms, the results. As expected, when processing motivation is low, we found that the condoms were evaluated more positively when respondents were in a positive mood compared to when in a negative mood. This result is consistent with the affect-as-information hypothesis that predicts mood-congruent evaluations under conditions of low processing involvement.

For the *textual* advertisement type, additional planned comparisons showed that evaluations in the high-involvement condition (when affect priming *and* cognitive tuning were assumed) were significantly more positive than evaluations of the condition where no mood effects were expected (the low-involvement, negative mood condition). Moreover, mean evaluation of conditions where mood effects were expected as a result of either affect-as-information (low-involvement, positive mood condition), affect priming (high-involvement, negative mood condition) or cognitive tuning (high-involvement, negative mood condition) did not differ significantly from each other, suggesting mood effects in these three conditions.

For the *visual* advertisement type, which had no text at all, a significant mean effect of mood was found. Participants evaluated the brand of condoms more positively when in a good mood than in a bad mood. Importantly, the interaction effect was not significant. This suggests that, as expected, when people do not have any argumentative message available to elaborate on, their evaluations do not become more positive when in a negative mood. As expected, evidence for affect priming (high-involvement condition) and affect-as-information (low-involvement condition) were found, but not for cognitive tuning.

Also as expected, when processing motivation was low, we found that the new brand of condoms was evaluated more positively when our participants were in a positive mood than in a negative mood. This was the case both when our participants were confronted with a textual ad (including relevant message arguments) as well as with a visual ad (with no message arguments included). This result is consistent with the affect-as-information hypothesis that predicts mood-congruent evaluations under conditions of low processing involvement.

Interestingly, we found no difference in evaluations between mood conditions when respondents were highly motivated and when they were presented the textual ad.

194

- (12): What we can learn from blood donation and Flexus condoms

When advertising a product that has negative connotations, one should take into account consumers' motivation to process the message. If consumers are likely to be only slightly motivated, one should advertise in a "positive atmosphere." Conversely, when consumers are expected to be highly motivated to process the message, both positive as well as negative atmosphere can improve evaluations.

To put it briefly, when one wants to advertise a product or a service that has some negative connotations, one should take into account consumers' motivation to process the advertised message. If consumers are likely to be only slightly motivated (as is often the case when consumers are, for example, watching a commercial block that interrupts a movie), one should advertise in a "positive atmosphere." Conversely, when consumers are expected to be highly motivated to process your message (as when you advertise a new car to automobile freaks), both positive as well as negative atmosphere can improve evaluations. However, if managers opt for a "negative atmosphere" (e.g. a commercial after the daily news or a sad movie), they have to make sure they have sufficient and convincing message arguments available.

Although not supported by the results of our visual ad type, we still cannot definitely exclude that the "null" effect in our high processing motivation and textual ad condition was due to processing motivation on its own, and not to different mood mechanisms (affect priming and cognitive tuning). After all, we did not find a pure effect of mood in this condition.

This would mean that our affects are not due to mood, but to increased cognitive elaboration by itself. To exclude this possibility, we again need to take into account some process measures, to find out whether or not our mood manipulation has an (indirect) effect on consumers' evaluations. Both affect priming and cognitive tuning are expected to lead to an indirect effect of consumers' moods on their evaluation, by influencing the thoughts consumers have while looking at the ad.

In a further study, we will investigate the assumed presence of both affect priming and cognitive tuning under conditions of high elaboration. We will take into account some process measures (e.g. the positivity of respondents' thoughts) to distinguish between a mood-based or an involvement- (motivational-) based account.

- (13): Affective state induced by ad-elicited affect instead of mood

Contrary to the two foregoing studies, we will approach the consumers' affective state by inducing ad-elicited affect instead of mood. We would like to argue that both lead to comparable affective valence effects. We should again observe more positive evaluations when mood is positive compared to when mood is negative, i.e. affect-as-information.

Our third study was designed to further investigate the effects of affect on the evaluation of a product category with negative connotations: meat. In recent years, most European countries suffered from meat crises that generated a lot of negative publicity.

The purpose of this study is to further test our already partially supported assumption that there are two mechanisms responsible for mood effects under conditions of high processing motivation: affect priming (if mood is positive) and cognitive tuning (if mood is negative.)

When mood indeed has an effect on evaluations when processing motivation is high, it is expected that both positive affect (affect-priming hypothesis) *and* negative affect (cognitive-tuning hypothesis) will influence the proportion of positive thought people will have, and a mediation analysis should indicate that mood has a direct effect on people's evaluations through the thoughts they have.

Contrary to the two previous studies, we will approach consumers' affective state by *inducing ad-elicited affect instead of mood*. While we acknowledge that both affective states (mood and ad-elicited affect) are not perfectly comparable, we would like to argue that both lead to comparable affective valence effects.

If the results of our first two studies are valid, then we should again observe more positive evaluations when mood is positive compared to when mood is negative (i.e. affect-as-information.) But when motivation to process is high, we expect no difference between the evaluations in the positive and negative mood condition: when mood is positive, we expect that positive affect will spread towards related positive constructs, making evaluations more positive (i.e. affect priming). At the same time, negative affect will enhance message scrutiny, such that elaborations in the negative mood condition will also become more positive (i.e. cognitive tuning).

- (14): Dual role of affect under different conditions of processing motivation

Results of the meat advertisement. We expected that positive affect would prime related positive material, resulting in more positive evaluations, i.e. affect priming. At the same time, we expected the contrary, based on the cognitive tuning hypothesis. In reality, we found evidence only for our cognitive-tuning hypothesis.

The results provide evidence for the dual role of affect under different conditions of processing motivation. Two of the modes address when affect has an impact on judgment, and two address when affect does not have an impact.

In what we call "heuristic processing," affect influences judgment because people use their affect as a shortcut to infer their evaluative reaction to the target. In what we call "substantive processing," affect influences judgment through its selective influence on attention, encoding, retrieval, and associative processes.

In essence, these two processing modes tell us that affect can influence judgments under low-processing motivation conditions by serving as a peripheral cue, and under high elaboration conditions by biased thinking.

Unexpectedly, we found mood-incongruent judgments in our high-processing motivation condition. On the basis of our assumptions, however, we expected no difference in evaluation scores between our positive and negative affect condition. This is because we expected that in our positive affect condition, positive affect would prime related positive material, resulting in more positive evaluations (i.e. affect-priming hypothesis). At the same time, we expected the contrary, based on the cognitive-tuning hypothesis. In reality, we found evidence only for our cognitive-tuning hypothesis: that is, only when felt affect was negative did we found more positive evaluations.

A possible explanation for the lack of affect priming in our high-processing motivation condition could be that the mental schema of meat was too negative for positive activation to be spread toward related constructs: we were in the middle of the meat crisis.

As for negative affect (cognitive tuning): careful consideration of the pros and cons (as a result of increased elaboration) was very likely to result in more evaluations that are positive. After all, given all the crises, there was a need for more quality control with regard to meat consumption.

• (15): Some simple lessons we can draw from all this learning

When they have to tell (and sell) "bad news," marketers should carefully choose an ad that elicits positive affect. Informational ads should be persuasive, since these arguments color thoughts and influence judgment. One should also take into account the consumers' level of involvement.

If a marketer wants to promote a product that automatically activates a negative schema—e.g. genetically manipulated food—choosing between an informational and an emotional ad will have serious consequences. Emotional and informational ads both elicit different processing styles.

If one chooses an emotional ad, one can best use an ad that elicits positive affect. In this instance, the positive affect in the emotional ad will result in more positive evaluations of the genetically manipulated food. This is because an emotional ad is less likely to call for detailed and systematic processing.

If an informational ad is chosen, both positive and negative affect can elicit more evaluations that are positive, if a number of conditions are met. If the mental schema (genetically modified food) is extremely negative, there are no related positive associations where the positive affect can spread—i.e. affect priming under positive mood conditions.

If this is the case, one can best use negative affect. Since negative affect evokes message scrutiny—i.e. cognitive tuning under conditions of negative mood—one can best make use of strong, pervasive, and very persuasive message arguments, since these arguments color thoughts and influence judgments.

Marketers should also take into account the consumers' level of involvement or processing motivation. Low involvement in the persuasion process calls for a positive approach, since affect as information (typically associated with low involvement or low processing motivation) results in mood-congruent evaluations.

On the other hand, if one is highly involved in the persuasion process, at least for product categories with a negative valence, it does not seem to matter much whether one is in a positive or negative mood. Both seem to elicit more positive evaluations compared to a more neutral mood condition.

Some considerations however . . .

- (16): Some considerations to make these simple lessons complete, or selling bad news is not always as simple as it looks . . .

However, one should make sure that the product category is not extremely negative if one deals with positive affect, otherwise the positive affect cannot be spread towards associated positive beliefs. If one deals with negative affect, one should have strong arguments: a negative mood indeed causes higher motivation to process, resulting in increased scrutiny of the message.

If a marketer wants to promote a product that automatically activates a negative schema, he or she should:

(a) make sure that the product category is not extremely negative if dealing with positive affect; otherwise the positive affect cannot be spread towards associated positive beliefs or constructs, and

(b) rely on strong and pervasive message arguments if dealing with negative affect, since people will base their evaluations on the strength and persuasiveness of the arguments that are being presented.

In summary, when one has to deal with products or services that have negative associations, the effects of mood depend upon a number of conditions. First, if people are not very motivated to process (the ad, the arguments), it seems that positive mood, or positive affect, leads to corresponding positive evaluations (i.e. mood-corresponding evaluations). Second, if people are motivated to process (as when the product is very important to them, for example) both positive and negative mood seem to enhance product evaluations. Positive mood (or affect) causes a spread of activation towards related positive constructs. This makes it important that there are positive constructs available. It is assumed that this is not the case with very negative products—for example, meat for a vegetarian. Negative mood causes a higher motivation to process, resulting in increased message scrutiny. It is therefore important to provide strong and pervasive message arguments in these conditions.

References

Callebaut J. (1996). Never too late to grow old, Censydiam Institute.

Callebaut J. & friends. (1997). Cross-Culturally Correct Marketing, Censydiam Institute.

Callebaut J. (2000). El Nuevo Modelo Diagnóstico Para El Márketing, Louvain-Apeldoorn, Garant & Censydiam Institute.

Callebaut J. (2000). Understanding Chinese Consumers, Louvain-Apeldoorn, Garant & Censydiam Institute.

Denzin, N.K., & Lincoln Y.S. (19998). The Landscape of Qualitative research, Theories and Issues. Newbury Park CA, Sage Publications.

Dichter E. (2002). The Strategy of Desire, Transaction Publishers.

Gaus, H. (1999). Gedragsfunctionalisme als methode van waarneming en als aanzet tot verklaring. Demokritos. Mededelingen van de Vakgroep Politieke Wetenschappen, Universiteit Gent 1999-4.

Gaus, H. (2001), Why Yesterday tells of Tomorrow, Louvain-Apeldoorn, Garant & Censydiam Institute.

Peter, J.P., Olson & Grunert K.G., (1999). Consumer behavior and marketing strategy, Maidenhead, McGraw-Hill.

Pettyn R.E. & Cacioppo, J.T. (1986). Communication and persuasion: central and peripheral routes to attitude chage, New York, Springer-Verlag.

Hirschman, E.C. & Holbrook, M.B. (1992). Postmodern Consumer Research, The Study of consumption as Text, Newbury Park CA, Sage Publications.

Beckmann, S.C. & Elliott R.H., (editors) (2000). Interpretive Consumer Research, paradigms, Methodologies & Applications. Copenhagen, Handelshojskolens Forlag. Oxfordshire, Marston Book Services.

Schwartz S.H. (1992). Universals in the Content and Structure of Values: Theoretical Advances and Empirical test in 20 Countries. Advances in Experimental Social Psychology, 25, 1-65.

Strauss, A. & Corbin J. (1994). Grounded Theory Methodology. In Handbook of Qualitative Reseach, Newbury Park CA, Sage Publications.

The Authors

Jan Callebaut

Jan Callebaut (born Geraardsbergen, Belgium, 1955) is a Diplomatic Scientist with a specialized licentiate in Marketing and Distribution. Jan Callebaut has developed several research techniques for the psychoanalysis of consumer behavior by applying the views of Freud, Jung, and Adler. After several years of experience in market research for various companies, he and Hendrik Hendrickx founded Censydiam. Jan Callebaut is the author of the Censydiam Institute publication *Never Too Late to Grow Old*, a psychological whodunit about motivational research among golden agers.

Madeleine Janssens

Madeleine Janssens (born Herentals, Belgium, 1959) is a sociologist and also took the postgraduate course of specialized licentiate of Marketing at the University of Ghent. Since joining Censydiam 1986, she has been active in the field of qualitative diagnostic research, two years of which she spent in the Netherlands. She has managed the Qualitative Research Division in Belgium since 1991 and currently heads the Censydiam Health Division specializing in pharmaceutical and health issues. Madeleine Janssens is co-author of the Censydiam Institute publication *Facing Arab Women*.

Hendrik Hendrickx

Hendrik Hendricks (born Antwerp, Belgium, 1950) is a psychologist who developed unique research techniques for the statistical measurement of psychological phenomena in consumer research. During his twenty years of professional experience in research and marketing, he worked as an advisor for various marketing companies before joining Jan Callebaut in founding Censydiam. In 1997, Hendrik Hendrickx inaugurated the new chair of Consumer Psychology at the State University of Ghent in Belgium for this newly recognized branch of psychology.

Diane Op de Beeck

Diane Op de Beeck (born Antwerp, Belgium, 1962) studied Communication Sciences and has fourteen years of experience as a market researcher in the United States, Indonesia, China, Australia, and just about everywhere in Europe. She has a keen interest in cross-cultural research, and is the author of a chapter on *Laughter in the West and in the East* in the Censydiam Institute publication *Cross-Culturally Correct Marketing*. As director of the Censydiam Institute, she now coaches new project leaders of different origins, a position that has taught her to approach cultural differences with a smile of empathy.

Brad Bortner

Brad Bortner (born Chicago, Illinois, United States, 1961) is the Managing Director of Censydiam's newly expanded US office in Boston. He has spent over twelve years focused on revenue enhancement, marketing strategy, implementation, and market research on both the client and provider sides. His approach stresses linking research insights with actionable recommendations. He has special expertise in bringing new products to market and repositioning products in newly competitive markets. His degrees include an MBA from Yale University, an MA from the University of Toronto, and a BA from Dickinson College where he graduated with honors.

Helmut Gaus

Helmut Gaus (born Heideck, Germany, 1942) is doctor of Modern History and a professor in the Faculty of Social and Political Science at the University of Ghent in Belgium. For more than 25 years, he has been making comprehensive studies of the subconscious motives underlying the behavior of large groups and masses. Research into the system and consistencies of underlying motives has made it clear that people are being influenced by cycles of increasing and decreasing uncertainty, which bear a close resemblance to the known long waves in economics. This is the basis of *Future Watch*, which he developed in collaboration with Censydiam.

Christophe Fauconnier

Christophe Fauconnier (born Ghent, Belgium, 1967) spent his childhood and early youth in South Africa. You could call him a South African Belgian or a Belgian South African. As a psychologist and economist, he has both the business and human sense to extend Censydiam's experience to more than 75 countries, working himself in more than 35. As a white South African, he knows that good judgment is impossible without knowing the context of the individual being judged, no matter which cultural background he or she may have. We thank him for contributing his insight to the chapter on *Cross-Culturally Correct Marketing*.

Anick Bosmans

Anick Bosmans was the first student to take her doctoral degree of Applied Economics under the guidance of the Research Centre for Consumer Psychology and Marketing. The research center was established to further the study and dissemination of insights from Economic Psychology. It is a joint initiative of Censydiam and the Marketing and Industrial Psychology departments of the University of Ghent, scientifically directed by the Marketing departments of the Universities of Ghent and Louvain. Anick Bosmans is currently research fellow at the University of Tilburg in the Netherlands.

Jan Pollaerts

Jan Pollaerts (born Dendermonde, Belgium, 1938) is a philologist who has devoted himself to semiotics, which he likes to define as the study of an aspect of culture as a formal system of signs. Before writing for Censydiam, Jan Pollaerts worked for a French news agency as a foreign correspondent in the Middle East and Asia where he covered social and cultural subjects. He co-authored the Censydiam Institute publication *Facing Arab Women* along with Madeleine Janssens.